Louis S. Davis

Studies in Musical History

Louis S. Davis

Studies in Musical History

ISBN/EAN: 9783337084813

Printed in Europe, USA, Canada, Australia, Japan

Cover: Foto ©Thomas Meinert / pixelio.de

More available books at **www.hansebooks.com**

STUDIES

IN

MUSICAL HISTORY

BY

LOUIS S. DAVIS

NEW YORK & LONDON

G. P. PUTNAM'S SONS

The Knickerbocker Press

1887

INTRODUCTION.

In presenting this little book to the public, I am actuated by the belief that it treats of subjects and periods of musical history with which the general reader is far from familiar. The voluminous character of Dr. Burney's and Sir John Hawkins' histories of music are well calculated to damp the zeal of the most ardent disciple of the tone art, nor does a chronological presentation of lives and facts offer any concrete view of the subject. Some men there are, who through their vast power of individuality have left their impress indelibly graven upon the art, and these stand out like beacon lights along the path of history; but their names are few, and it is with periods and institutions that we have to deal. Upon him who, in the succession of the centuries, does not observe the sequence of cause and effect, the lessons of history are wasted, and its example thrown away. Say not "Lo here, or lo there," but laying a firm grasp upon the salient points, by a synthetic process arrive at the inner comprehension of the whole.

He who narrates facts without deducing principles, discovering analogies, or tracing causes, is no historian; and while he may furnish ample data for the use of others, he is at best only a compiler. The history of music furnishes no exception to the universal law, and the intention at least of this work is to present facts in a philosophical and homogeneous manner. Since it is to the Church that modern music owes its existence, it is from the history of the Church that much of this volume is drawn. Music is but one of the effects of the great cause, the Christian Church, and upon its rituals and institutions depended the fate of the whole tone system. Whether we consider the Mass of the Catholic Church, or the Choral of the Church of Luther, we see that each has builded its part well, laying a firm foundation for the universal temple of spontaneous utterance, where all alike may worship in catholicity of belief, which knows no law but that of perfect harmony.

CONTENTS.

STUDIES IN MUSICAL HISTORY.

CHAPTER I.

A STANDARD OF MUSIC.

THROUGHOUT the vast fields of art or science there is no department which possesses so remarkable a combination for refining and instructing as that of music. The word standard draws the clear-cut line between the work of the conscientious student and that of the time-server. In every department, whether it be that of medicine, painting, law, literature, sculpture or mathematics, a high standard of excellence is demanded, and in most cases satisfactorily accorded. Nowhere should this requisite obtain with the same inexorable severity as in music. One great difficulty in the way of a popular and correct conception of music, is that we are not wont to regard it as we do anything else, but put it aside with the feeling that it is so much a part of another world from ours, that it would be impossible ever to get *en rapport* with it. On the contrary the tone realm is only one of the great parts which make up the great whole in nature's intellectual laboratory. A good composition has as clearly defined

I

a plot as any work of fiction; it is as logical in its development as the profoundest treatise; its rhythms are as varied and rich in their meanings as the most complex of modern poems. Its proportions must be as perfect and its shading as delicate as the most carefully designed work of the painter's art. Always, however, with this exception, that while the painter, sculptor, or author at best only reproduces objects and characters from real life, the musician, from the unseen, unknown, unseeable, unknowable, evolves combinations of sound for which there is no counterpart, unless it be the unseeable and unknowable, which, in a man's nature, is hidden inscrutably from himself.

I have spoken thus of the character and principles of music in order the more clearly to demonstrate the absolute necessity for a fixed standard in this, as in any other department of art or science. If we admit that one composition is superior to another, we, by that admission, acknowledge the possibility of an unlimited number of degrees of merit, and come again to the original necessity—a standard.

True, the composition of a high order is frequently, in the popular vernacular, too scientific, too hard to understand. There is a demand for something simpler, not thereby meaning a fresh and childlike simplicity such as is found in " *Volklieder*," but rather a demand for a certain kind of maudlin sentimentality, such as the popular ballad, at once the cause and effect of such unwholesome and unpleasant emanations. This, the result of an ignorance of music, vaunted as though it were a virtue; or a yet more deplorable kind of ignorance, which supposes its pos-

sessor not only a musician, but a critic of no mean
capacity. Without doubt there is a distinct tendency
in a musical utterance to morality or to immorality,
as may be expressed in more familiar or definite
forms. Here, as elsewhere, the standard of right and
wrong must be fixed. And now we are confronted by
two questions which must have suggested themselves
from the start : What shall the standard be, and who
shall enforce it ?

First, as to the standard. Adhering to the principal parallels in substance and degree in all departments of thought, I find nothing which more fully
illustrates the world of music than the world of literature. Only a few examples may be cited, but they
are so mutually reciprocal in their plan and mode of
thought, their orbit is so essentially one, that the most
incredulous must admit that I am advancing something more than an hypothesis. In a certain sense
all literature is true, and in the same sense all music
is true. But there are some truths to which we attach
greater importance than to others. There are some
truths which it is not only idle to discuss, but which
it is best not to discuss at all. Among great thoughts,
what is there more similar than a Bach fugue and
an essay by Mill. In both cases we begin with the
subject, then its developments and train of inductions
and corollaries, its culmination and triumphant conclusion. Who tells best the lives of such men as
" William the Silent "? Beethoven, in his " Symphony
Heroical," or Motley, in his " History of the Dutch
Republic "?

It would be difficult, if not impossible, to find in all

the German schools of philosophy a transcendental
mysticism more profound than that which pervades
and saturates every page of Robert Schumann.
Dramas there are in Chopin, crowding a whole life's
story into an interval not greater than fifteen minutes.
As in literature some history becomes romance, and
some romance history,—we know not where to draw
the line,—so in true life, the intellectual is so clouded
with the keenest and most subtle appreciation of the
beautiful, that we draw the line nowhere, saying this
is such and such, but rather leave that to the sentiment and interpretation of the artist. It will thus be
seen that a good standard of music neither limits the
field of taste nor the mood of the individual, rejecting
only that which is condemned by the unerring laws
of harmony as laid down by our greatest musical
authorities. It now remains to find an agency powerful enough and sufficiently omnipresent to make *musicians* in every village and home in the land.

The worst feature of the case is that before supply
we must create a demand, and this on a scale commensurate with the vastness of an American popula-
tion. If the United States Government had the power
and the will to attempt such a creation, no effort on
its part, no matter how strenuous, would avail except in
isolated instances. But the Central Government has
neither the will nor the power to inculcate art, and it
is not to it that we can look. Conservatories founded
by individuals must, through their incapacity to reach
the mass, fail to make ours a music-loving people.
America for her musical instruction must look to the
greatest and most universal educator that the world

will ever possess—the Christian Church. She, who for upwards of two thousand years has been the guide and schoolmaster of Europe, is the only power which could make this or any other a music-loving people. The larger number of our greatest musicians and composers have come to us from the Old World, through the doors of the sanctuary.

Two hundred years ago, two great and typical men were born into the world, and those two men were called John Sebastian Bach and George Frederick Handel. What the Church did for them they tried to pay back to the Church. How well they met their obligation the Church knows better than any one else. Indeed, there is no branch of education which has so faithfully, and in so spiritual a manner, endeavored to recompense their mother and teacher, the Church, as that of music. So, admitting that the Church has been the greatest patron and benefactor of musicians, we must also admit that the musician has been the greatest beautifier of her rites and services, giving her a high spiritual standard of music, which in this country, however, is but little known. I believe that no one will dispute that whatever is intended for a sacred purpose cannot be of too sacred or elevated a character. If music is essential in a church, it should be of as pure and devotional a character as possible. But in the majority of churches it is so tawdry, frivolous and commonplace that to be a Christian and a musician rather partakes of the nature of a paradox. The dignified and intelligent calling of the musician, the sacred and responsive position of the organist, are unrecognized by the public at large. There is a remedy, but

to get at it we must go to the fountain-head. How
shall a minister know if his church has a good standard of music unless he has been instructed in music?
In suggesting this, I do not propose a course of counterpoint and fugue for the theologue, but a theoretical
course which shall enable him to distinguish good from
bad in music as in theology, and to know a sound musician as readily as he would a sound theologian.
Another point now presents itself,—the musician's pay.
In this country, where we hire music-teachers as we
do serving-girls, and organists as we do blacksmiths,
these callings receive pay proportionate to the respect in
which they are held. A competent minister commands
a proportionately good salary, and a good musician
should be recompensed according to his competency.
If a congregation gets good preaching, or good playing
for a trifle, they have, through the necessity of the individual, gotten that for which they have not made an
honest equivalent. The minister who permits his organist to receive only a pittance is aware of one of
two things—either, that the organist is worth only a pittance, or that he and his congregation are what in any
other calling would be denominated " beating down,"
and that, for the best of reasons, because they can. The
brain-work of the educated musician is as great as that
of a minister, and his physical labors are greater. The
Protestant Church in this country is degrading rather
than elevating the standard of music. First, through
the musical ignorance of her ministers; and second,
the trifling inducement which it offers for good music.
   The rule of values which holds good in all else, does

not hold here.   In most cases an organist is not chosen
by virtue of any talent or education he may possess,
but by reason of being a member of a particular church
or because he is in needy circumstances.   This last is
most frequently the case, and is the clearest indication
of the slight respect in which music and musicians are
held, when an organ becomes nothing more than the
means of an act of charity to one individual.   Ministers are never employed as a matter of charity; why
should organists be?

Charity is a noble action, but a charity which denies
a rightful salary to a legitimate musician to give a
pittance to an incompetent person is an economical
perversion of the eleemosynary spirit, a degradation of
music, and an offence against the Church.   I have
heard these cheap organists improvise during the service such doggerel, as in more musical communities
would have been considered rather bad for a hand-
organ.   There is a retributive justice in the fact that
it is the nature of men to give the last word an undue
importance.   I have known the effect of the most elo-
quent and solemn preaching neutralized, if not dissi-
pated, by the slap-dash jig which let the congregation
out of church, and spoke of anything but the just
finished sermon.   The position of organist is a very
responsible one.   He should be *en rapport* with the
minister; he should have the capacity to re-echo his
words.   His position confers a great, but unrealized
power, for good or evil, and this consideration makes
the responsibility of selecting an organist a very grave
one.

Before closing, I wish, in order to prevent any misapprehension of the object of this paper, to indicate some of the offences of the average cheap organist and repeat my suggestion of a remedy. The head and front of their offences against God and man is the ridiculous and monstrous practice of improvising on all occasions. Four-fifths of these persons could not make a practical application of a rule in musical theory. Three-fourths could not name the simplest rule, and two-thirds never heard there were any rules; and yet they improvise. The reason for this abnormal tendency lies in the fact that very few of those who play on organs are acquainted with or capable of playing legitimate organ-music. To play organ-music requires that *both feet* shall be used with equal dexterity, and as *legato* on the pedal-board as both hands on the keyboard. It would not be unnatural to suppose from the staccato pedalling, that these organists had at one time been engaged in a great war, and had each had a right foot shot off, but that the same right foot is kept see-sawing on the pedal which opens and closes the swell-box of the instrument, the object of the swell being to increase or diminish sound at the exact passage where each would be most effective. But the see-saw with the swell-pedal becomes a habit with the one-footed organist, ceasing to produce any effect but that of monotony. What opinion can we have of an individual who, having the whole world of the greatest organ-music to choose from, prefers to enthrall his audience with his own inspired drivellings?

There is in proportion to the number of performers, more good music written for the organ than for any instrument in the world. Suppose that any person of ordinary musical talent should call together an audience and improvise for their delectation on the piano,. violin or any other instrument, how long would it be tolerated? Yet in the performance of the most sacred office of music, this impertinence goes unchallenged. How many organists could plead guilty of knowing even the names of such men as Best, Schneider and Ritter? If the manner of considering could in any degree express the real value and importance of the matter considered, it would not fail to lead to salutary results.

To sum it up in a few words, music is an intellectual, refining and humanizing influence. A standard is just as much needed in music as in any other department of thought and feeling. There can be but *one* standard, and this founded upon authorities of so high an order as to preclude any question of reliability. The only power which could fix such a standard is the Church. This can be done by making a theoretical course in music a part of a theological course, which must create a demand for good organists; and as the organist, by reason of his selection of an instrument, is of necessity a better theorist than any other musician, he will be able to impart a fuller knowledge of his art than is now customary.

From the Church would go forth in this country, as in other lands, a high musical culture, which would return to her an hundred fold, giving her a new life in the birth of congregational singing, and giving her anthems the dignity and holiness which they have in the Old World. Here is nothing impracticable.; and while such an organism would necessarily take years to ripen to maturity, its result would be certain, and its effect durable and glorious.

CHAPTER II.

SPIRIT OF JEWISH MUSIC.

IT is not at all remarkable that music of some kind should have been known in ages almost pre-historic ; for, as a tone is, after all, only a prolongation of sound on any one degree of the chromatic scale, the human race could not have been very old before some individual made this discovery by blowing through a tube. Whether the tube was the throat or a piece of bamboo the difference was only in the timbre. The wonder, therefore, is not that music should have been discovered, but that the human race should for four thousand years have lived with the knowledge that there was a tone-world without the ability to enter it. There are, of course, sufficient reasons for this crystallizing, chief of which is the lack of mechanical appliances which, in our day, have made of such instruments as the piano and organ a marvel of ingenuity, power and sweetness. Still less a matter of wonder does it become when we remember that the knowledge of steam and electricity as active and tremendous forces were realized long before any glimmering intimation of the science of music ; and yet it remained for Handel to write his Messiah while the forces which now shake the world still slept, nothing more than a perception, a realization which had existed from the earliest breath of the race.

With regard to ecclesiastical music, or indeed music of any kind, the first authentic information of which we are possessed comes to us from the land of the Pharaohs. On the banks of the Nile, history has carved in characters of stone the achievement of this early civilization, giving ample record of the respect in which music was held, and the importance attached to its performance in all religious rites. Barbaric as must have been its character, not only on account of the primitive nature of the instruments, the thin, disconnected harmonies, the poverty and attenuation of melody, there is that seeking for the ethereal, that feeling for the beyond, which gave to tone-history a beginning that, through all the ages of waiting, held fast the promise of its immortality when its laws should be comprehended, and the union of tone and spirit become forever one and indivisible.

When Verdi wrote that superlative anachronism, the opera " Aida," he unconsciously performed an act of poetic justice. The scenery, the costumes, the instruments, yea, even the tombs, are all there with the studied exactness of detail, harmony and chronology, which reveal the hand of the archæologist wherever the curtain rises. Suppose that, instead of the voluptuous, almost lurid splendor of the music, we would substitute the ancient Egyptian mode of clothing thought in tone, how inexpressibly flat and meaningless it would then appear. Yet the fruit which Verdi plucked sprang from the seed planted on Egyptian soil four thousand years ago, and amid the tombs and temples, the groves

and palaces of the land of the Nile, we hear the evolutionized echo of the tone-life of pre-historic man.

Under the religious despotism of Egypt ecclesiastical music arrogated to itself and maintained an importance which has left its traces on the manners of
the people of that country to-day.   Where the temples
of Luxor and Carnac rise in pyramidal majesty, amid
the pomp and splendor of Thebes, sang the mighty
army of the priesthood.   No organ there ·to shake the
vast halls and open courts with the thunder of its
double diapason, or weave its colossal harmonies in
sympathetic utterance with the surrounding immensity,
but a voice which spoke of a faith as supreme and gi-
gantic as the autocracy under which it governed a nation of slaves.

And these slaves,——

Here, amid scenes of grandeur, which to-day, with the
everlasting solitude brooding among its sphynxes and
its columns, with its ritual forever departed, amid its
stones standing stripped of their wealth of gold and
ivory, precious wood and precious stones, appals the
modern traveller with the sense of its sublimity and of
his littleness here at the summit of Egyptian power,
and in the midst of a ceremonial conducted nowhere
else, since man drew breath, on so vast a scale, lived
and listened to the hymn of religion and of despotism,
a nation at once slave and alien.   The Jew might look
and listen, but he looked for a deliverer and he listened for his voice.   In the choral thunder of the
Egyptian priesthood he heard only the prayer of idola-
try and the voice which governed him by the power of

the lash. In despite of four centuries of slavery, the polytheism of the land of his adoption had taken but little hold on the heart which cherished the remembrance of the God of Abraham. The unifying power of the Pharaohs stopped short when it encountered the unit of Goshen. Here, as in subsequent ages, they might murder his children and hold him and his people as the property of the Government, but behold the limit.

Few as were the traditions possessed by the Jews at this time they, nevertheless, sufficed to maintain them an unbroken phalanx against every disintegrating external agency. But with that remarkable race-capacity for discriminating, and the no less remarkable ability to assimilate, it was not strange that, rejecting the dominion of Egypt, they should have retained for their civil and religious code a compilation largely based on the law of their taskmasters. Thus it was that music also became incorporated into their ritual, never to depart from it while Israel should be Israel. On the banks of the sacred river, beneath the shadow of the pyramid, within the precinct of the walls where the names of Isis and Osiris were uttered with reverent and bated breath, and in the lowly dwelling of the slave, Israel had sung his lamentations and songs of bondage. But the hut and the temple were alike to disappear to give place to the arch of heaven, and the hymns of bondage to be substituted by anthems of freedom and victory.

And now begins one of the most remarkable and sublime successions of composers of religious psalmody whose history was ever recorded by the pen of

man. From the day of the Exodus until the close
of the Old Testament history there passes before
us in an almost unbroken procession, judges, kings,
prophets and priests, who were in the loftiest, broadest and profoundest sense the greatest of poets to
which the race has ever given birth. From this day
Jewish psalmody, with its concrete immensities of
thought, was to be the foundation of all ecclesiastical
music. By the law of repetition we find men of the
nineteenth century deriving strength from the hymns
which, more than three thousand years ago, gave inspiration and endurance to the Jewish people in their
life-and-death struggle.

Under the theocracy founded by Moses, ecclesiastical music was a term synonymous with national music.
Of all influences to which humanity is susceptible, those
of religion and patriotism are, I think, the most powerful and enduring. Moses was perhaps the only man at
that epoch who could gauge the dynamics rendered
possible by such an union. Filled with assurance that
the God of Battles was with him, and nerved and stim-
ulated by the thought that the eye, not of his General,
but of his General's General, was upon him, the defence of his home and the honor of his God were so
blended into one, that, to the Jew, a victory over an
army of idolaters was as much a religious rite as the
ritual of the tabernacle. Thus it was that every patriot was a religionist, and every true religionist was a
devout patriot. As in the case of the galvanic battery,
the closing of the circuit between the positive and negative poles makes known the presence of the electric
current, so it was that the completion of the circuit of

positive and negative religion and patriotism, through
its very intensity, produced a current of thought whose
vibrations shall continue to be felt when perhaps the
name of the people from whom it sprung will have
passed into oblivion. The text remains, but the music
was oral, as in the case of all preceding and most of
the following music in every land.

It is believed that many of the melodies now in use
in the Jewish ritual have an origin pre-dating the
Christian era by some centuries. But as for this claim
there is no verification ; it must always remain an open
question. Nor have we, as in later periods, the means
of estimating the growth and development of ancient
Jewish music, either as an art or an auxiliary to ecclesiasticism. There is indeed a comparative method by
which may be guessed the character of Jewish music
at the time of the Christian era; but this process would
only show that melodies now in use are either of a
comparatively recent date or have been so chromat-
ically altered as to render them past recognition save
by the student of the old Greek modes. The difference in these modes, or scales as they are now called,
lay, of course, in their succession of tones. They had
not, as we have, major and minor scales, but differed
from us in having one to suffice for both. Thus the
Dorian mode, corresponding to our key of D (of which
the Phrygian and Lydian, with all their derived keys,
were but transpositions, as in the case of the modern
scale), differed from our scale of D in that its third,
sixth and seventh were made minor. With this explanation I trust I shall be more fully understood when I
repeat that, although there may exist Jewish melodies

to-day which were written prior to the Christian era, their identity is so veiled or lost by chromatic alterations as to be almost unrecognizable.

These primitive modes continued during some centuries of Christian music, and, indeed, are still found in the old Gregorian chants and German chorals. That there were many instruments, and many kinds of instruments, is a fact patent to the most casual reader of either sacred or profane history, but their compass and scope was limited, and they, if not from choice, from necessity were subordinated to music of the voice. As from the storehouse of Egyptian wisdom the Greek and the Jew had alike derived all that was known of music, so in a later period was Christianity to build on their work, and to fashion its hymns and chants upon the harmonies and melodies which lineally descended from the music of the Pharaohs. While Christianity, in its musical heritage, owes no more to the Jew than to the Greek, so far as real tone-knowledge is concerned, inasmuch as it first had being on Jewish soil, incorporating the Old Testament belief with the New, we may readily believe that where Jewish theology expounded the doctrines of the Christian, Jewish music would early be adopted as his psalmody.

There remains a noble, but as yet unwritten chapter, which shall one day place music before the world as one of the great factors which go to make up history. Mighty weapons are the battle-hymns of Jew and Christian, Catholic and Protestant. You can hear them through all the ages that have been, clear and strong, forever welling up from the heart of the nations. And whether these be hymns of peace or hymns of war, songs of grief or gladness, they are insensibly and imperceptibly fashioning the history of the race. This is, to my thinking, a field of speculation which to a careful student might yield a rich harvest. So far as I know, it is a subject which has never been directly discussed, but the time will come when we shall realize the great historic importance of ecclesiastical music..

2

CHAPTER III.

"And when they had sung an hymn they went out unto the Mount of Olives."

TWELVE men are sitting at a table; they have just engaged in a rite of the significance of which most of them are unaware. These men are willing but unconscious actors in the great drama just about to commence. These are not, as they once were, rude, ignorant fishermen and artisans, drawn from the Jewish peasant life. Three years ago they *were* such, but with such a teacher and such an example they had learned to grapple with the problems of here and hereafter, and to love all humanity as their neighbor, and their neighbor as themselves. As their subsequent history proved, three years had made them thinkers and logicians. To-day they have signed their faith in the blood of the grape; hereafter they shall seal that faith in a redder and a warmer libation. Reverent, yet bewildered, they sit about the table in that upper chamber. They do not know it, but they have just been partakers in the most potential rite ever celebrated. There was still a veil between them and the Master. They must have been seated a long time, for the night has come down, and outside they can hear the shouts and songs of the rejoicing people,

gathered in Jerusalem for the Feast of the Passover.
It was a large room where they sat, and through the
open windows (for it was the warm Judean spring time)
they could see the blazing fires around which the
people gathered in preparation for the feast. *Their*
feast is over, and they have been sitting perplexed,
grieved and wondering, while they listened for the last
time to the words of their beloved Teacher, Master and
Friend. And now they have eaten the bread and
drunk the wine.

"And they sang an hymn." In all history I know
of few sentences which convey more than this. It is
the adoption and endorsement by the Christian Church
of psalmody, and through it of ecclesiastical music.
Doubtless that hymn was sung by all the Christian
Church, and it is not improbable that that very melody
still lingers in the form of some old Gregorian chant,
its identity forever buried and lost. What would the
Church *not* give to sing the, at once, communion and
crucifixion hymn its Master and Founder Himself
sung? Sing it now, Apostles, as you sit about the
Master, with the blood of the grape upon your lips.
But the day *will* come, when, amid the flames of
martyrdom, or the agonies of crucifixion, that hymn
will rise, consecrated by a deeper meaning, and a
memory which can never perish. Simon Bar-Jona,
thou shalt sing that hymn, the memory of thy denial,
repentance and forgiveness ever before thee, as they
carry thee to thy crucifixion in the Eternal City.
Andrew, thou shalt sing that hymn in the day that
they raise thee on the cross, which shall ever be known
by thy name. Beloved disciple, in years to come,

amid the lonely exile of Patmos, with the vision of a new heaven and a new earth stretching out before thee, the girdling ocean shall hear thy poor, old, quavering voice, singing this communion hymn in loving retrospection.   Look, James, thou just man, on the people who keep the Passover to-night, for one day, with this hymn in thine heart, they will stone thee to death in this very city.   Bartholomew, fifteen hundred and thirty-nine years hence, in the year 1572, 30,000 innocent men and women shall lay down their lives in thy name; but this posthumous crime shalt not be laid to thy door, and thou shalt bear thy gospel, thy hymn and thy cross to the far off land of India. The man Judas, who solved the great problem by fulfilling the Scripture, was not there; had he been, that memory might also have gone with *him* to a death of glorious martyrdom, in years to come.

What a fathomless profundity there is to a chorus of men ! How like the ocean ! How earnestly and how devoutly do they sing this first recorded Christian hymn ! How their voices blend and swell out on the warm fragrant air of the spring night.   In Ephesus, in Smyrna, in Pergamos, in Thyatira, in Sardis, in Philadelphia, in Laodicea, the echo of those voices will be heard. And it will be sung alike in the dungeon and in the catacombs.   And wherever this hymn is sung the Apostles will say: "In the very hour that made us a unit in faith, *He* sang his farewell hymn."   Every memory of the past fades into nothing in the light of the intense reality of the present.

This hymn is consecrated, and by *its* consecrating power, *all* hymns are made consecrated.   Put out the light and add to the gloom of your souls the darkness and gloom of the silent Gethsemane. But the hymn has only paused, and when it comes again upon your lips the night will have passed away, you will sing it in the blazing glory of the noonday sun.

A NOTE.—"There is some ground for believing that this may have been the series of Psalms called Hallel (cxiii. to cxviii. of the Authorized Version), which was used in the Second Temple at all great festivals, and consequently at that of the Passover; and it has been supposed—though the circumstance does not admit of proof—that the melody to which the most characteristic of these Psalms, *In exitu Israel,* was originally sung, is the germ of that with which it has been associated in the Christian Church, from time immemorial—the Tonus Peregrinus."—PURVIS' "Dictionary of Music."

CHAPTER IV.

THE MASS.

No matter how involved in mystery and obscurity, the contemplation of any long period is always impressive. Music as an art does not address itself to the average historian as does painting, sculpture and the like.

Of the early history of Christian music there was but little to be said, and of that little but a small portion has come down to us. Hymn-singing as practised by Christ and His disciples was, as was the custom among the Jews, confined to chanting the Psalms of David. . Tradition is silent as to how long this custom continued, but with the new faith there arose the necessity for distinctive Christian psalmody.

While among all nations the recognition of rhythm is the rudimentary form of music, in spite of the slight knowledge of melody possessed by the early Church, rhythm was excluded from all sacred music. Added to this arbitrary and unnatural practice was the use of the old modes, which, rugged and impressive, convey a sense of austerity and gloom which left its traces and bore its fruit in after centuries. Until recently, music, as understood in the modern sense, had no existence. Harmony was unknown, counterpoint was undreamed of. The compass of every scale or mode was very small, rarely exceeding two octaves. The variety of instruments was few and their capabilities slight. The knowledge of all these things was wrapped in the un-born centuries, and while it waited all Christendom was lulled by the monotony and awed by the severe sim-plicity of the chant soon to be known as the Gregorian. It is indeed a tall tree which for centuries reaches upward without even branching; but the taller the tree, the nearer the sun. What a long time to wait, what a long way to go; but through the dense growth of ignorance and depravity this slender shoot held its own, feeling for the light and only finding it with the dawn of the Renaissance.

There are two men to whom, musically speaking, the world can never pay its debt of gratitude; and of these two, differing so essentially as they do, the most remarkable fact is that their greatest work was not that of music, nor was music made a specialty with either, nor is the difference in their theology greater than the times in which they lived. When Gregory ascended the pontifical chair civilized Europe was reeling under the repeated blows of barbarian inva-sion, and was preparing, not metaphorically but liter-ally, for its plunge into the Dark Ages; and through all that time the chant that forever bears his name went on, its ceaseless murmur growing with each successive century, and wherever its voice was heard there was also the uplifted cross and the gorgeous ceremonial of the Mass. Near a thousand years elapsed between the days of Gregory and those of Martin Luther. Throughout all that period the people learned slowly, and by imperceptible degrees, as much by hereditary transmission as by individual absorption, acquiring not a musical education but a musical sense which in due season was to bear fruit, and in Luther's German choral take the highest musical step ever accomplished by the body of the people.

Men are not naturally musical, and like a good many lessons taught by the mediæval Church, without it the knowledge of music would, most probably, be still in its infancy. In all that period of ghastly gloom and grovelling ignorance, no matter how mistaken the policy of the Church, it was she who preserved the love of the beautiful in every department of art. Ignorant folk like little children remember better for pictorial illustrations. Through all Christendom the love of the mild, gentle mother with the infant Jesus in her arms appealed to the hearts of the people, and from the thing symbolized they turned with adoration to the symbol. Thus there went on an insensible process of education, and a sense of all that is beautiful in painting, sculpture and music grew in the hearts of the people at large. Much has been said of that unprecedented development of the knowledge and culture known as the Renaissance, and but little of the long planting and careful watering by the only universal educator of all the Dark Ages. In the case of music the result was more marked than in any other, for Greece and Rome had left their undying models of beauty, and they, not their memory, are with us even unto this day, but the music of the ancients could not even be called elementary, and one great work which the Roman Church all unconsciously performed was the preparation of a rich soil whence should spring a new art and a universal language. Without the Church there would have been no need for the organ, as it was only required for sacred choral music; and without the organ the growth of harmony must have been long delayed, and without harmony there is no music.

The gradual growth and development of the ritual known as the Mass is the subject embodying more musical interest than any other work of the Middle Ages. The result of this growth was an overwhelming pomp and splendor well calculated by its appeal to every sense to both dazzle and enthrall. Through necessity, the services of the early Church were conducted without either bells or instruments. Of the origin of the Mass there is great uncertainty, but I quote from an accepted authority in the Catholic Church, and without comment. "The opinion is sustained by the ablest liturgical writers that it was St. Peter, the prince of the Apostles and head of Christ's Church, who said the first Mass, and this after the descent of the Holy Ghost in the very same cenacle at Jerusalem where the blessed eucharist was instituted, and where our Lord uttered the words, 'Do this in remembrance of me.'" The note says, "The cenacle which stands upon Mt. Sion is to-day one of the greatest objects of veneration in the Holy Land. It is remarkable as being the supposed place where the Last Supper was held; where our Lord appeared to his disciples after his glorious resurrection on Easter morning; where the sacrament of penance was first instituted, and where our Lord was seen to converse for the last time with his chosen band before he ascended into heaven. It was in this blessed spot also that St. James the Less, styled the brother of our Lord, was consecrated first bishop of Jerusalem; and a pious tradition has it that it was here the beloved disciple said Mass in the presence of the blessed Virgin, who, it is said, departed this life there." I have quoted the above in full because the institution of the Mass, no matter where or at what date, was a matter of paramount importance, musically and otherwise.

The consideration of the Mass leads us into that of a ritual as little known outside of the Catholic Church as is the modern ritual of the Hebrews. While this discussion involves nothing of the Mass but its music, it yet necessitates distinctions and a presentation of data having no direct musical bearing. Through sanction, custom and tradition the rite of the Mass is not, as is generally supposed, the same either in the substance of its prayers and chants and in the order of their succession. Besides the different rites of the Eastern Church, there are in the Latin Church alone six in number of such rites which come within the sanction of the Church. They are the Carthusians, Carmelites, Dominicans, Mozarabics and Ambrosians or Milanese. Another erroneous general impression is that the language in which the Mass is conducted is exclusively Latin. While this is to a great extent correct, there is a minority of churches where Latin is not used, and where the ancient and obsolete vernacular is the vehicle of rendition. These languages are Greek, Syriac, Chaldaic, Sclavonic, .Wallachian, Armenian, Coptic, Ethiopic and Latin. It is of course of this last, the Latin Mass, that I shall speak exclusively, and that, not as it may have existed in its stages of growth, but as it stands to-day, elevated and adorned by the hands of the world's greatest composers.

It would be an impossibility to enter into the spirit of the music without being governed by the same influences and the same underlying meaning of the Mass proper which swayed the composer, as it would be to comprehend its language without any knowledge or translation. Like every great text, that of the Mass has been Vandalized by hundreds of composers both ignorant and shallow, but the mention of such names as Mercadante, Millard, and the like of our own day and generation is enough, and we are glad to leave their consideration to the attention of their numerous admirers.

The more we regard the difference in the periods in which Gregory and Palestrina lived, the less are we able to form an estimate as to the relative value and merits of their ecclesiastical music. A loaf of bread in a starving city is worth more than a barrel of flour in the midst of plenty. Certain it is that without a Gregory there could never have been a Palestrina, and regarded in the faint and uncertain light of that period Pope Gregory the Great must be considered the father of modern ecclesiastical music. Before his time, St. Ambrose instituted the chant still known by his name ; but of these chants only one or two are still in existence, and no matter what their merit, they were either absorbed in the Gregorian or lost in the process of the ages. One of the first acts of the Church after it became dominant was the establishment at Rome of a school of ecclesiastical music.

What and how much that school taught will never be
known.   As there was no system of notation, figures
alone were used and these were subjected to laws of
tone-inflection, the knowledge of which has long
perished.   Pope Gregory conferred a great benefit
on music by applying the same Roman letters to
denote all the replicates of the same sounds in different octaves.   Before his time, it appears the sounds in
the double octave or great system of the Greeks
had been denoted by fifteen Roman letters.   Gregory
reduced them to seven, applying the same letters in
different forms to three octaves, and while in notation
they have been superseded by the line and space,
have yet given names to our modern scale.   There is
a fascination in dwelling upon the manifold labors of
Pope Gregory, and in tracing their subsequent results
both direct and indirect.   For three hundred years
after his death the school which he founded in Rome
flourished, doing honor to his name, bearing in every
land fruit in testimony of its founder's greatness.

The incomparable superiority of the music of the
Mass over all other liturgical music, such as that of
the Church of England, for example, resides in the
principle that music can only present one idea clearly
at one time, and as in the liturgical anthems of the
Protestant Church the only idea is to get over as many
words as possible in as short a *space* as possible, the
music generally means nothing, or else attempts to
mean so much that the average intellect becomes ex-
hausted in the struggle after an intelligent hearing.
Try and imagine a Haydn or a Mozart writing a
Gloria in Excelsis on one or two pages.   In Haydn's

first Mass in B flat the Gloria covers eighteen pages,
Novello's edition ; and in his third Mass in D the
Gloria covers sixteen pages, and the English translation
in use in the Episcopal Church is an exact counterpart of
that sung in the Mass. If churches *will* have liturgical
services and they cannot afford time for the musical
development of the text, then, rather than use the
unutterable bosh with which most of our church services are disgraced, better sing nothing but the plain,
quiet old chants, and in their dignity express the reverence so seldom found in the so-called anthem used
in the Protestant liturgy. The same words which
when read or spoken many times in succession appear
not only meaningless, but foolish, when illustrated
with music assume a deeper meaning and a firmer grasp
on the imagination with every repetition of the phrase.
Thus it is that in Haydn's third Kyrie of eight pages
the great cry, " Lord have mercy upon us," " Christ
have mercy upon us " (following as it does that majestic prelude which in itself seems to lead Elijah-like up
to some lofty Carmel), bursts out with a spontaneity
and vehemence which gathers force and dramatic
energy as it proceeds. Twenty-seven times is it repeated, and with the last phrase we feel that we have
only now arrived at the full meaning and comprehension of the text. If the Protestant liturgist should
still object to "vain repetitions," let him call to mind
that in the Benedicite omnia opera Domini, sung in
the Episcopal Church every Sunday during Lent, the
words, "Bless ye the Lord ; praise Him and magnify
Him forever," are repeated thirty-one times, and then
ask himself what is the difference between a frequent

repetition of the words " Kyrie eleison," or " Bless ye the Lord; praise Him and magnify Him forever."

The Mass is in substance the Oratorio of the Messiah on a reduced scale. As in Handel's oratorio, the Kyrie represents the waiting, fear and expectation, leaving behind it the feeling that the answer is not far off. When miracle plays were common the Gloria in Excelsis must have presented a far more vivid picture than now; for the people had seen the shepherds abiding in the field, and the great light that " shined round about them," and heard the burst of angel music proclaiming, " Glory to God in the highest, on earth peace, good-will to men." But with Palestrina or Haydn to interpret he must be poor indeed who cannot see the picture and hear the voices. The Gloria is generally written in three numbers, and both it and the Credo for artistic purposes answer every requisite. In the case of both, the subjects are so arranged that the second or middle movement presents an antithesis to the first and third. To this fortunate accident is due some of the finest effects which the Mass presents. Of the origin of the Gloria as a whole there is no certainty, all that can be said being that the anthem as it now stands was composed by some of the Drs. of the Church. Of the origin of the Credo there is certainty, it having been adopted by the Council of Nicea, when it superseded the creed, known as the Apostles' Creed.

There is a tradition which, from its quaintness, I cannot refrain from quoting. At the end of the missal of St. Columbanus, an Irish saint of the sixth century, there is a very curious tract on the creed, which, among other things, assigns the portion composed by each of the Twelve Apostles. The order is as follows :—

"First, St. Peter: 'I believe in God the Father Almighty, Creator of heaven and earth.'

"Second, St. John: 'And in Jesus Christ His only Son, our Lord.'

"Third, St. James: 'Who was conceived by the Holy Ghost, born of the Virgin Mary.'

"Fourth, St. Andrew: 'Suffered under Pontius Pilate, was crucified, dead and buried.'

"Fifth, St. Philip: 'He descended into Hell.'

"Sixth, St. Thomas: 'The third day He rose again from the dead.'

"Seventh, St. Bartholomew: 'He ascended into heaven and sitteth at the right hand of God the Father Almighty.'

"Eighth, St. Matthew: 'From thence He shall come to judge the living and the dead.'

"Ninth, St. James, son of Alphæus: 'I believe in the Holy Ghost.'

"Tenth, St. Simon Zelotes: 'The holy Catholic church, the communion of saints.'

"Eleventh, St. Thaddæus: 'The forgiveness of sins.'

"Twelfth, St. Matthias: 'The resurrection of the body, and the life everlasting.'"

It is difficult to discuss the Credo without viewing it from a comparative standpoint. Both the Credo and the Gloria begin with an announcement. The first, "Glory to God," the second, "I believe." The first conveys tidings, the second announces their acceptation. Both are triumphant, the one in giving, the

other in receiving.   The first is a rhapsody of mingled
prayer and thanksgiving ; the second formulates Christian belief and tells the story of its origin.   The inco-
herent ecstasy of the one is fully made up by the
lucid exactness of the other.   Without the Credo, the
Gloria would be incomplete.   It is so freighted down
with the great tidings that it has no room for explanation.   A man who had never heard of Christianity
would learn very little about it from reading only the
Gloria.   The Credo succeeding it becomes at once its
exponent and commentator.   The triumph of the
Gloria, and the exultant confession of the Credo; the
one to be followed by a prayer, the other by the story
of the manger, the passion and the cross.   The Gloria,
anticipating the recital of the Credo, cries out, " Thou
that takest away the sins of the world, have mercy
upon us."   The Credo, in the same antithetical spirit
exclaims, " He became incarnate of the Holy Ghost,
of the Virgin Mary, and was made man."   At the
words, " Et incarnatus est," the people as one fall
upon their knees and so remain till " Et homo factus."
    The tender, loving manner in which this second
movement of the creed has been dwelt upon by every
great composer by whom it has been set, gives ample
testimony to the powerful and dramatic appeal to the
imagination.   At the words " Et sepultus est," the
whole picture of the garden with the tomb hewn in the
rock, the weeping women, the darkness, the sacred
hush of the just-dawning Easter day, and above all
that intensifying sense of sympathy in all the congregation, imparts to the individual a feeling of vivid
reality which acts alike upon composer and auditor.

if the " Qui tolis " of the Gloria is absorbed in prayer,
Ihe " Et incarnatus " of the Credo is lost in contemplation. From the first we are roused by the words " For
Thou only art holy ! " From the second by the trumpet call : " The third day He rose from the dead ! "
In the one the hymn of triumph is resumed ; in the
other the climax of Christian belief has been attained.
Standing now, as it were, at the end of these two anthems, we feel that they are indeed finished, and that
the appointed time for the great Amen is at hand.
Amen, amen, amen.

Following the Credo at different intervals, there are
four short movements. The Sanctus, the Benedictus, the Agnus Dei, and the Dona Nobis. The impression which these convey is one of perfect rest and
tranquillity. · Only twice is this feeling broken, and
then not in a manner calculated to jar. This when, at
the end of the Sanctus, the voices swell again into the
old clarion, " Hosannah in Excelsis," and again at the
end of the Benedictus when the same refrain is taken
up. With the Credo we reach the dramatic climax
of the Mass, and from that time on the spirit follows
willingly down to the peaceful sunset of the " Dona
Nobis Pacem," and in the quiet radiance of that peti-
tion for peace the music of the Mass is ended.

One object in thus dwelling upon the music of the
Mass is, as at first stated, with the intent to show the
difficulty if not impossibility of, for instance, setting
such an anthem as the Te Deum Laudamus to music
limited to five or ten minutes. In so doing, I have
been careful to make the distinction between the liturgical and the non-liturgical music ; for outside of the

3

Mass, all the good sacred music is unconnected with a liturgy, and this for the reason that the smaller the text the more of a unit will be the composition. Mendelssohn, Bach, Handel, these are the men who made one text cover a multitude of pages. Every composer of sacred music is quite as much an expounder of a text as a minister; and if a minister finds it a logical impossibility to preach from twenty different texts, how then can he expect a musician to write logically or rationally on more texts than he himself can develop. One other reason for reviewing the entire music of the Mass is that it is my wish for clearness to treat of it once and for all, and I consider that no better or more proper place could be found for such consideration than in connection with its founder, the great Gregory.

CHAPTER V.

FROM the days of Gregory until far into the eleventh century the history of music is a blank. Those four centuries were very busy ones to Christendom, and so far as music went, its cultivation was at a standstill, and the best the monasteries could do was to take care of what had come down from Gregory. Society had not to be reformed, but to be created. Alaric, Attila, Genseric all have their will, and the carnival of massacre and ruin shrouds the proud empire forever from view. And now the conqueror is to be conquered, and the religion of the vanquished is become the religion of the victor. In the midst of chaos is heard the trumpet of the soldiers of the Crescent, and not for the first time the fortunes of the Cross tremble in the balance, but the blows of Charles the Hammer fall thick and fast, and the battle of Tours sends the Moslem host back over the Pyrenees. The struggle is from within and without. Every monarch is a despot, every lord follows his master's example. Feudalism and serfdom are the order of the day; and lo! in the midst of conflicting forces a cry is raised, and, as a man, Europe springs to its feet and rushes in maddened disorder to death, and to save for Christendom

35

the sepulchre at Jerusalem. These were no times for music or for art of any kind.

I have digressed in this manner because without considering the nature of the forces with which Europe was shaken from the seventh to the eleventh centuries it is impossible satisfactorily to account for the utter stagnation of everything musical. I do not mean to say that there was no music during all this time, but it has left no record; and as it comes once more into view shows little if any progress. There were secular melodies, but they were tolerated rather than approved by the Church. Charlemagne, it is true, amid the manifold cares of his empire, was careful to have compiled a book containing all the songs of the people then in use, but by the ungodly zeal of his successor this book was destroyed as having a sinful tendency. In another chapter I have endeavored to show that the growth of the church organ was the forerunner of the study and practice of harmony. This growth had by imperceptible degrees proceeded, and men, by using both hands, began to find out how much better was the sound of an octave than of one single tone, and after awhile, though with less good reason, how much better it was to add fourths and fifths, thus at least presenting a framework to be indeed both added to and altered, yet giving the first impetus in the growth and development of modern harmony.

About the middle of the eleventh century there arose two men, Guido of Arezzo and Franco of Cologne, who by their discoveries and inventions made progress in music practicable. Guido was the first to employ any system of notation with a staff. Franco wrote a treatise on harmony which in those days of obscurity served as a guide-book to his successors for two centuries. Guido also introduced what is known as solmization or singing by syllable, afterwards to form the foundation, and in many cases the material, of the German choral. He was led to this innovation by observing that in the hymn to St. John the first and middle syllables of the first three lines formed a regular ascent in the scale of the major mode, as we should say. This hymn is preserved, and, as connected with an invention which is still in practice in most countries in Europe, we consider it a curiosity worthy of being presented to our readers.

> "Ut queant laxis
> Resonare fibris
> Mira Gestorum
> Famuli tuorum,
> Solve polluti
> Labii reatum
> Sancte Johannes."

Thus was brought into use that vocal scale with which we are all so familiar : do, or ut, corresponding to our c, and the remainder of the scale, re, mi, fa, sol, la, the si or b in Guido's system being omitted.

The next work of importance is the treatise of Marchetto of Padua. He wrote about the end of the thirteenth century. Between the time of Franco and that of Marchetto an immense amount of unpreserved work must have gone on, for when he wrote the old system had undergone many changes. In his book there is found a thing never known at any previous time—modulation and the use of the sharp. In the fourteenth century there lived one John de Muris, a

native of Normandy. Dr. Burney says, " His art of
counterpoint, though comprised in a very few pages,
is the most clear and useful tract on the subject which
those times can boast." For the rules contained in
this most excellent little work I refer the curious
reader to the Edinburgh Encyclopædia, page 44.
Before his time there had sprung up the system for
regulating time in music, a thing hitherto unknown.
It is said to have begun about the time of Guido, but
wherever it came from it was long in reaching perfection. John de Muris' work for the first time gives examples of harmony which are not calculated to offend
the ear, and is another of those broad steps on which
the tone-system was slowly mounting.

About the end of the fourteenth century musicians
began to depart from the measured feet, that is, the
equal values of Guido, and to introduce different values,
that is, the quarter, eighth, sixteenth, etc. Fifty years
later there arose another John, called Tinctor. This
man wrote the first musical dictionary. After this it is
easy to imagine that the facilities for acquiring music
were mightily increased. Franchinus speaks of only
five characters for time : the maxima or large, equal to
our whole note, the long or half, the breve, the semi-
breve and the minims, or sixteenth ; but other writers,
early in the sixteenth century, added to these the
crochet, the quaver and semiquaver. Tinctor, already
mentioned, founded in Naples the first musical con-
servatory ; and coincidently Willaert, another Fleming, founded one in Venice, their object being, as implied in the definition, to conserve the art of music
trom corruption. This was the signal for other similar

institutions in different parts of Europe, but it became the fashion wherever there was the newly-revived study of the classics of Greece and Rome, to have a chair of music, thus early in the history of modern European music giving it an equal place with the highest departments of thought.

Notwithstanding the Italian schools of which Rome formed the centre, the great drift of musical invention and genius seems to have passed at this time to the Netherlands. Neither space nor interest admit of more than a passing notice of all these really great men. With the beginning of the fifteenth century we see the names of John Okenheim, his scholar, Josquin des Prez, who was deservedly recognized by his contemporaries as the greatest musician of his day, Henry Isaac, Jacob Horbrecht. All Europe, Italy not excepted, sat at the feet of the Netherlands, and they furnished masters to every country. Adrian Willaert, a Fleming, was the head of the school of Venice, and wrote a valuable work on musical theory. But the greatest glory of the Lowlands was in giving birth to Gaudio Mell. It was he who instructed the young Palestrina, thereby giving to the world the greatest revelation of music it had as yet received.

About the middle of the sixteenth century the rage for ostentatious, intricate and over-crowded harmonies had reached its climax. Pedantic adherence to rules rapidly becoming obsolete, together with a mania for all kinds of ingenious and grotesque figures thrusting themselves in on all possible and impossible occasions, rushing madly hither and thither, the great point with each composer seemed to be to see how many hair-

breadth escapes his manifold parts could make by just
avoiding a collision. Under this state of things the
musical solemnity of the Mass was gone.   At what
period for high days the Gregorian chant had been laid
aside for music of a more rhythmical character is not
known, but certain it is that at the time of Palestrina,
so far from being a step forward it had reacted upon
itself, and what had once promised to be the greatest
musical blessing had now become the greatest musical
curse.   In place of reverence and devotion, the music
now caused nothing but amusement and distraction
from the services of the Church.   Pope Marcellus II.
had a bull prepared, and was actually on the point of
its publication, banishing from the Church all music,
most probably with the intention of a return to the old
chants upon which the Church had relied for so many
ages.

I regard this as one of the most important crises in the
history of music, for had the Roman Church banished
all but the old chants the consequence would have
been of a far-reaching character, and might have had
results which will readily present themselves to the
historian.   It was at the earnest prayer of Palestrina
that the bull was held in abeyance until he could write
a Mass such as he considered to be in accordance with
the spirit of the sanctuary.   His music was constructed on an original model, and although he has
been surpassed by more modern Mass writers in dramatic intensity, nowhere has he been surpassed either
in purity of harmony or in the perfect spirit of sincere
devotion.   Like David, Gregory inaugurated the work
for the building of the great temple; and though many

ages lay between them, yet, like Solomon, Palestrina was to make good the promise of his predecessor.

With Palestrina the daylight of music may be said to have fully broken. We have traced it from the banks of the Nile, and accompanied it as it went out with the triumphant hosts of Israel. We have followed it through the wilderness and its dwelling in the Holy Land. We have listened to its voice as it floated out on the air of the spring night in commemoration of the right which it would ever be its privilege to glorify. We have followed it as it followed the cross from land to land, and have seen the barbarian hosts bow down in dumb wonder before an influence and a sensation never before known. Ambrose, Gregory, Guido, Franco, Marchetto, Muris, Tinctor, Okenheim, Des Prez, Isaac, Horbrecht, Palestrina, ye are all dead, yet living. The graves which hold you can never hold your memories, and the music which you loved has gone out to all the world in commemoration both of you and of your religion.

For more than thirty-five centuries the art had awaited recognition. It had seen every other liberal art rise to a climax of perfection, and then decay. There are many trees which require a number of years before bearing, yet having once borne they continue to do so long after their earlier bearing contemporaries are dead and forgotten. As though seeking retirement behind every barrier which nature could interpose, there stands in Calaveras County, California, a group of trees the like of which the world has never seen. There they stand, mountains of everlasting green. Four thousand years have left four thousand rings in

their massive trunks, telling the story of an unprecedented and a green old age. By its side the oak
might flourish, dwarfing into nothingness the little
slender shoot of green ; but the oak reached maturity,
grew old, decayed and fell, and the shadow of its
smaller companion lay across it. Ages passed away
and oak followed oak to the cemetery at the feet of
the big trees of Calaveras, and to-day these trees stand,
fit emblems of an art which has for four thousand
years reached forward, imperceptibly growing and
standing alone as the one art without precedent and
without approximation.

History is full of great peaks where the student may
pause, and in a general retrospect, take in all the
journey that has been accomplished; and it is to such
an eminence that Palestrina carries us. Many of · the
rules under which he worked have since been declared
without harmonic foundation. Innovation after innovation has drawn a broad line of demarcation between
the music of Palestrina and that of the present day.
The world has grown rich in a vast variety of instruments possessing an almost unlimited compass. Orchestration has been born and reached maturity, counterpoint has had its rules so immovably fixed as to
render it most improbable that they will ever be super-·
seded. The history, the philosophy, the beauty of
music have all been dwelt upon by men whose whole
lives have been given up to the one end—the glorifica-
tion of their art; but to one man, and to one man
alone has it been permitted, once and for all, to draw
back the curtain which should unveil the stage of tone-
life to mankind forever and forever.

The age of Palestrina is noteworthy not only as ushering in a new era of music, but also in its secularization and general diffusion among the masses. Strange to say, this result was brought about by the creation of the oratorio. "From a very early period music had been employed to enhance the effect of the sacred plays, and as it continued to occupy the same position when the drama had been secularized, St. Philip Neri, in 1540, in order to counteract the new attraction, originated at Rome the oratorio. About twenty years later, Palestrina, the chaplain of the Vatican, reformed the whole system of church music. These exertions would perhaps have retained for it something at least of its ancient ascendency but for the invention in 1600 of recitative, which by rendering possible complete music dramas, immediately created the opera, withdrew the sceptre of music from the Church, and profoundly altered the prevailing taste. From this time the star of St. Cecelia began to wane, and that of Apollo to shine anew." That such was the case can be a matter of regret to no unbiassed mind. The capabilities of music are so inclusive that to have pent its great overflowing in one channel would have dwarfed into comparative insignificance the most expressive art ever yet developed. The average opera is at best but a poor educator for musical taste, but as a stepping-stone up and into the tone-life, it has been of vast importance. Not only was the great work of music henceforth to lie outside of the church, but ecclesiastical music itself was to experience changes and divisions hitherto unknown. At the beginning of the seventeenth century, the musical drama and the orchestra were unappreciated forces, but in their growth we can trace the growth of every other form of secular music, and it is to them that we must continue to look for the education of the people at large. I have said that church music itself was to experience alterations and sub-divisions, and it is with an unmixed pleasure that I now turn to the representative school of Protestant choral music.

CHAPTER VI.

CHORAL.

IF Palestrina may be said to have fulfilled the Gregorian promise, how much more may it be said of John Sebastian Bach, who developed every line of music proceeding from Martin Luther and his school. To Gregory and to Luther was it given to plant, but to Palestrina and to Bach was accorded the privilege of reaping. What Palestrina did for the Mass, Bach did for the German choral. Of the comparative work of the two men, that of Bach stands pre-eminent, and not only by comparison with Palestrina, but with all contrapuntists. As in the case of Gregory and Palestrina I shall review that of Luther and of Bach from an historical rather than a musical point of view. Of the underlying theological causes which gave weight and impetus to these two great movements, this work has nothing to do; but if, at some future period, the historian should trace an analogy between the music of the Reformation and the spirit which gave it being, I consider it safe to say that that analogy will not be far to seek.

Bach's development of the German choral has so immediate a bearing on the invention and growth of counterpoint and fugue as to render a brief consideration of the departments a necessary introduction. The

45

first name which appears in this connection is that of John Dunstable, who died in 1453. He is said to have been the originator of florid counterpoint. Considering the low standard of musical taste now existing in England, it is a matter of surprise that that country in time past has accomplished so much for music. "In the meantime instrumental music, properly so-called, began to improve. Ludovico Viadana, if he did not invent, was at least the first who drew up general rules for the figures of Thorough Bass, and composed an organ bass differing from the voice part. Girolamo Frescobaldi, of Ferrara, who flourished about the beginning of this century (that is, the seventeenth) composed fugues expressly for the organ which were admired and imitated all over Europe. His Ricercari, etc., were among the first compositions printed in score and with bars. Ricercari and Fantasie preceded sonatos and concertos, and were the first compositions expressly made for instruments after the invention of counter point."

For fourteen centuries the people had listened to the chanting of monks, and had on all occasions been silent participants in the services of the Church. They had heard the Mass chanted generation after generation in a foreign and in a dead language. But with the birth of the Reformation, Germany burst into the vernacular choral which has never ceased from that day. I believe it is not too much to say that without the German choral the Protestant revolt against the Church of Rome would never have been permanent; and the hymns of Luther and his contemporaries occupy quite as important a place in history as gunpowder, printing, or any other prominent discovery or event. It was on that last battle-field on which he was ever to stand that Gustavus Adolphus gathered his 15,000 Swedes about him and all sang, " Ein feste Burg " and " Fear not, O little flock." The drums and brass instruments also played the hymns, and the field of Lützen trembled beneath the inspiration born of those never-to-be-forgotten chorals. Listen! on the shore of the Red Sea there stands a host. They have come out of bondage, and for the first time in 400 years they are a free people. It is the sister of the Lawgiver who sings. More than 3000 years lay between Miriam and Gustavus, yet the spirit of both hymns is essentially the same, and the inspiration derived from them nerved men to deeds of heroism, placing beyond a question the influence of the battle-hymn. Miriam sang, " Sing ye to the Lord, for He hath triumphed gloriously; the horse and his rider hath He thrown into the sea." Listen to Gustavus as he stands on the field of Lützen. " Ein feste Burg ist unser Gott.

> " A safe stronghold our God is still,
>   A trusty shield and weapon ;
>   He'll help us clear from all the ill
>   That hath us now o'ertaken.
> The ancient Prince of Hell
> Hath risen with purpose fell ;
> Strong mail of craft and power
> He weareth in this hour,
>   On earth is not his fellow.

> " With force of arms we nothing can,
>   Full soon were we down-ridden ;

> But for us fights the proper man,
>   Whom God himself hath given.
> Ask ye, who is this same ?
> Christ Jesus is His name,
> The Lord Zebaoth's son,
> He and no other one
>   Shall conquer in the battle. "

This is Carlyle's translation, and I cannot help adding his memorable words in commenting on this powerful choral. "The one entitled, 'Ein feste Burg,' universally regarded as the best, jars upon our ears ; yet
there is something in it like the sound of Alpine ava-
lanches, or the first murmur of earthquakes, in the
very vastness of which dissonance a higher unison is
revealed to us. Luther wrote this song in times of
blackest threatenings, which, however, could in no
sense become a time of despair. In these tones,
rugged and broken as they are. do we hear the accents
of that summoned man who answered his friend's
warning not to enter Worms in this wise :—'Were
there as many devils in Worms as these tile roofs, I
would on;' of him who, alone in that assemblage before all emperors and principalities and powers, spoke
forth these final and forever memorable words,—' It is
neither safe nor prudent to do aught against conscience. Till such time as either by proofs from Holy
Scripture, or by fair reason or argument, I have been
confuted and convicted, I cannot and will not recant.
Here I stand—I cannot do otherwise—God be my
help, Amen !'" If ever there were hymn and tune
that told their own story of a common and simul-
taneous origin, without need of confirmation by ex-

ternal evidence, it is these. To an extent quite without parallel in the history of music, the power of Luther's tunes, as well as of his words, is manifest after three centuries, over the masters of the art, as well as over the common people. Peculiarly is this true of the great song, *Ein feste Burg,* which Heine not vainly predicted would again be heard in Europe in like manner as of old. The composers of the sixteenth and seventeenth centuries practised their elaborate artifices upon it. The supreme genius of Sebastian Bach made it the subject of study. And in our own times it has been used with conspicuous effect in Mendelssohn's Reformation Symphony, in an overture by Raff, in the *Festouverture* of Nicolai, and in Wagner's Kaiser march; and is introduced with recurring emphasis in Meyerbeer's masterpiece of The Huguenots.

The German choral possessed two new features, which from the day of its birth gave it a hold on all classes. These were the vernacular of the text and the simplicity of the melody. Luther's second preface to the Funeral Hymns expressly states that many of the tunes of which he made use were taken from the music of the Mass, and as many of the chorals were in the old Greek modes they must have been a re-setting of the Gregorian chants. The difference in the chant and the choral being that in the chant many words were sung to one tone; whereas in the choral there was only one word to each tone. The difference between the German hymn and those of most other nations is to be found in the fact that the German chora is a succession of tones of equal value, and largely consisting of half and whole notes. The first of these

4

peculiarities makes the singing of the choral very easy to every congregation, and the second, by giving greater length to the tones, imparts weight and solemnity to every word of the text. Another inestimable advantage in having tones of equal value lies in the fact that only on such a succession of tones could those beautiful preludes known as choral preludes, have ever been founded ; for without notes of equal value it would be impossible for a composer to offset them with any given group of tones, or as musicians more commonly express it, to make a succession of any one musical figure.

Yet another peculiarity of the choral is that every tune has one text and no more. The absurd practice existing in all the American and English churches of singing from ten to a hundred different sets of words to one tune, becomes manifest if the same adaptations be attempted in secular songs. The gentleman who sang "O, all ye people clap your hands" to "Yankee Doodle" was not much further in the wrong than those who sing any other words to the Old Hundred psalm tune. As musically anything seems to be allowable in the average American church, this very serious defect, while it must always be deplored, cannot excite much surprise or wonder. In beautiful contrast to the Anglican hymn tune, the choral is always known by the first line of the text of which it is the exponent. When the English and Americans write a tune, it is never, and perhaps with very proper humility, considered worthy to bear the name of any text, but is generally named after some man or woman ; or if not, it is to be called Uxbridge, Manchester, Birmingham, etc. If the gentlemen who name these hymns intend, by so doing, to convey a healthy and salutary hint that the ways of man will not always be free from smoke, and by inference may come in contact with its possible cause, then we can find no fault with their most admirable, delicate, and altogether unobtrusive manner of inculcating a very important tenet.

Contrast the names of the German chorals with such as Cambridge, Duke St., Federal St., and Rockingham. This last is an offset to Maryal's Twickenham. The choral disdains a name. Its one text is good enough for it to be known by, and thus they are called, "Dear Heaven, behold," "Out of the Deep I cry to thee," "By help of God I fain would tell," "Now praise we Christ the Holy One."

In Germany children are taught to sing the choral just as they are taught to read and write. These hymns are the heritage of the people, and the school children know them, not by some irrelevant, meaningless title, but by that one text which they were intended to interpret.

One other feature of the greater number of the German chorals is that they are either in four-four or two-four time. The effect of every movement is dependent as largely on its time as upon its tempo or speed. The uneven accent attendant upon three-quarter time, except in rare cases, renders it an improper medium for hymnody. In the case of two-four or four-four time, the accent falls upon the first and second half of the bar, and in three-four time, upon the first beat alone. In the average hymn, the use of triple time produces an undignified effect which only unusual exigencies can justify. There are many texts to be found in our very best hymns which from their

rhythmic accent compel that found only in triple time.
A very few German chorals have found their way
into our hymnody, and the fact of the popularity of
such hymns as Dundee and Old Hundred shows that
the introduction of the whole Luther choral would be
by the mass of the people welcomed and adopted.

I am aware that this subject is not enough understood in this country to be popular, but before leaving
it there is one more characteristic to which attention
should be called. The introduction into the choral of
notes of equal value precludes in most cases the use of
dotted notes. A dotted note is usually followed or
preceded by a note having only one-third the value of
the dotted note, and makes that which should be beautiful and stately, both jerky and irrelevant. Added to
this, it has a decidedly secularizing effect upon the
music of the churches, and to one who was not familiar
with either of the melodies it would be difficult to say
which was the hymn and which the song, " Don't
Leave your Mother, Tom," or " O to be Nothing, Nothing." Music must do one of two things. It must
either ennoble or debase. If hymnody does not ennoble a service it must detract from it. In the chapter
entitled The Standard of Music, I have dwelt at such
length on this subject that in spite of my desire to do
so, I do not feel justified in farther enlarging upon it.
It is with pleasure therefore that I turn from such
names as Lowell Mason, Thomas Bradbury, the
Messrs. Root, which latter were generally impressed
with the necessity of hymn-writing at a very late hour,
and that they might inspire a due sense of their feeling on that occasion in the hearts of their adorers,

would write before beginning, "Midnight." Farewell, ye Lowrys, Doanes, Hulls, Shermins, Grannis, McGranahams, Bliss, Kirkpatricks, Sweenys.

Coming out of this somewhat unpleasant atmosphere it is blessed to look to the men to whom all ages must look for musical instruction and the everlasting out-welling of the true spirit of devotion. Luther was born in 1483; the great Bach was born in 1685, 202 years later. It was Luther who dedicated the choral to the German people, but it was the Thirty Years' War which consecrated that choral, sanctifying it with the best blood of the Fatherland. With Luther it was born in war; with Bach it was developed in the midst of peaceful contemplation and devout study. It is quite as impossible to discuss the German choral without a mention of Bach as it would be to discuss the Mass without the name of Palestrina, the symphony without Beethoven, the oratorio without Handel, the opera without Wagner, the dance without Strauss, the violin without Paganini, the string quartette without Haydn or Bach without the organ. The age of miracles can never be said to have fully passed away so long as men throw away and neglect many of the greatest acquisitions. To me the ignorance, indifference and prejudice which ignores and destroys appears, though in an inverted ratio of excellence, quite as marvellous as the creative fiat. Improbable as it seems, the day may come when the German choral shall cease to be the song of the people. Should such ever be the case, the people will deservedly have lost their birthright; but with the true musician such can never be. What Luther did for the people, Bach did for the musician.

Until a man shall arise who shall intellectually super-
sede Bach, he must always stand pre-eminent as a
composer. Through ignorance the mass of the people
is always more liable to let slip any manner of good
than men of real intelligence and education. Men
may play Bach without understanding him, but they
cannot understand him without being intelligent.
The choral took hold upon the people because it required no study for them to take hold upon it. Of
Bach it might be said that his preludes and fugues
appeal to the musician because they require severe
study; but no musician who has ungrudgingly be-
stowed this labor upon Bach can ever say that Bach
has proved himself ungrateful.

Bach's choral preludes in volume form a comparatively small part of his unequalled work, but when it is
remembered that the amount of that work already
published fills thirty thick volumes, and that there is
much more yet to follow, it is easy to see that what
was very little for Bach would alone have made any
other man famous. Those who wish for a condensed
and sympathetic insight into the work and excellence
of John Sebastian Bach can gratify their wish by reading the article by J. S. Dwight, published in the *At-
lantic Monthly* for June, 1885. Bach in his choral prelude was peculiarly fortunate, not only in his unlimited
imagination, fertility of resource, ingenuity, knowledge
of form and his intuitive selection of the exact material for the right place so that all things he did were a
structure builded of closely fitting stones, but in his
selection of the subject on which his preludes were
based. Bach himself wrote a vast number of chorals,

indeed some hundreds, and adapted and arranged many more. All this of course fitted him to select with perfect accuracy those hymns which in the prelude would most richly and abundantly develop. Complete and beautiful as was this department of his work, it was after all the power of association which gave to them the charm which they possessed for their Lutheran hearers. As every choral is known by its text, so every prelude recalled that text and the remembrance of it made the playing of Bach quite as much an act of prayer and praise as when the minister prayed or the people sang. The description of one of these choral preludes might be understood by one who had already heard them, but as it would be unsuccessful for one who had not, I forbear. Sufficient to say that they carry the melody of the choral throughout, only pausing now and then in order that the undercurrent of original subject-matter may round off a period in the melody, or introduce new contrapuntal material upon the resumption of the choral melody.

When Bach played, the congregation knew just when the choral theme entered, and where it paused. From their earliest childhood they had listened to these hymns. They had been part of their lesson at the village school, and later on they had joined in singing them with the whole congregation in the Sabbath Day service. How many sacred memories there are connected with the hymns in our own vernacular, yet we did not learn them in the company of our school-mates, the friends and companions of our early years; indeed only a few of them sing them, and of those who have departed this life our memory recalls

only a few who sang; and yet with all these disadvan.
tages, the association of the American hymn-tune is
one of the strongest which the Sunday service possesses. But with the Lutheran choral it is, or was,
different; but only in degree, for where we have one
such memory they had many. When men are stillest,
they feel most. When the lips are mute, the memory
is most active. Thus was it that with his congregation gathered about him Bach preached to them a sermon of memories. No sentimentality here, but a solemn
and tender retrospect. Listen! Bach is preaching :—" Frühmorgens, da die Sonn aufgeht " (Early in
the morning when the sun is rising). Bach is preaching:—" Wir glauben All an Einen Gott " (We all believe in one God). Bach is preaching :—" Ich ruf zu
dir, Herr Jesu Christ " (I call to Thee, my Lord and
Savior). Bach is preaching, and memory is preaching,
and it will be long before the memory of that choral
fades.

To any other man the creation of any of Bach's
masterpieces would have been an event of paramount importance, but to Bach such things were so
common that outside of getting married twice and having twenty children, his life was a strictly uneventful
one. Nor is there evidence that Bach himself considered these as possessing great merit, though from so
modest a man such an opinion of himself, if entertained, would never have been expressed. The town
of Eisenach, where he lived, did not know that he was
great, and when he died it seemed that his memory
had died with him. The world went on making new

musical combinations, and composers lauded themselves upon their originality, and the art rose to a high degree of excellence. Time passed, a hundred years went by, and the name of Bach was but little known. His works slept in the original manuscript form in the town where he had labored, and it must have been during this period that some, perhaps many of them, were lost. But like the good seed awaiting its time, Bach only slept. It was Mendelssohn who called him forth and said to the world, Where now is your boasted originality? No, they had not written one chord, nor made one combination which Bach had not made a century and a half before.

Since the days of Bach the market has been flooded with text-books. I do not think that Bach ever wrote a text-book, and yet it was he who showed the whole musical world every principle involved either in Harmony, Counterpoint, or Fugue. Handel was his greatest contemporary, and his work has been before an admiring public ever since its production; but Handel's pales before that of the long-forgotten master, and the tardy justice to the memory of the dead has come at last. Besides being the greatest authority on theory, Bach, so to speak, invented many new keys by making the temperament even in all the twelve major keys on the piano. Hitherto only three or four had been employed, but with the new temperament every tone in the system became available for a key-note. This is a subject which should be discussed at length to be made clear, and I hope that the opportunity may at some future time present itself for so doing. No

monument can ever be raised to the memory of Bach
half so imposing as that which he all unconsciously
erected. The world does well to honor his memory,
for in so doing it does unto itself the greatest of
honors.

CHAPTER VII.

To every man the power of leading, the power of sway-
ing, the power of controlling large bodies, is that qual-
ification which seems, for the time being at least, to
confer an inherent superiority over the majority of his
brethren. Successful or unsuccessful, as the result may
determine, the general leading an army to battle is, no
matter how small of stature, the very biggest object
there. There is a duple enjoyment of power, sometimes objective, sometimes subjective. There is always
as much pleasure in yielding to a sway as there is in
wielding it. In the crash of a thunder-storm, in the re-
sistless fury of a cyclone, the awful majesty of an earthquake, men stand bewildered and dumb, crushed by the
helpless terror of impotence. This is the power of
brute matter exercised for our ruin, from which we
shrink appalled. These are external. But the influences to which we gladly yield ourselves, are those
which appeal to our intellect or passions. The student
of moral philosophy might, and with good reason, discuss the latter, which of necessity debases energy;
but such is not my purpose here, but to confine myself
to the sway of intellect over intellect, not only from the
standpoint of the swayed, but in one particular case to
emotions of the swayer of men. The baton of the Ca-

pell Meister confers happiness on him, as does the
baton of the field-marshal.   There are bodies which
are neither human nor intellectual, yet confer a great
dignity upon him who by reason of hard study and inde-
fatigable labor has acquired their control.   There is a
dignity pertaining to the office of the man who, standing
at his key-board, draws out a message coming from the
other side of the world, and so places you in immediate
communication with your fellow-beings who live thousands of miles away.   There is a dignity pertaining to
the office of the smutty engineer as he stands at his
post, down in the great ship, and lays his hands on his
heart and sees that her pulsations are regular, and her
meat and drink always forthcoming, for we know that
if that hand pause the heart must stop, and the great
ship stand still.

But there is yet another kind of machinery and another kind of dignity to which we must now direct our
attention.   It is my wish to speak as briefly as possible
of the wonderful machinery of the organ, and of the
dignity and responsibility of the organist.   Like most
of our possessions, the organ has a pedigree which
reaches back where the memory of man runneth not.
Indeed, its father and grandfather are still with us, in
some out-of-the-way places, but of them I mean to
speak later on.   One writer has irreverently called the
organ the "*box of whistles.*"   Dr. Stainer, in his work
entitled "The Organ," has more accurately expressed
it as the "collection of flutes."   One flute was the beginning, two flutes was an improvement, three flutes
made a triad, and every additional flute gave greater
scope to the instrument and the player.   So far as is

known, the first organ had its being among the Chinese, and is called the Cheng. It is blown with the mouth and played with the fingers exclusively. Much research and erudition have been expended by modern scholars in the endeavor to trace the origin and history of the organ, but I believe that all that is known of any value on this subject down to quite a recent period is contained in the following lines, from Dr. Stainer's little book called "The Music of the Bible." It is generally said that they were introduced into church services by Pope Vitalianus in the seventh century. But on the other hand, mention is found of an organ which belonged to a church of nuns, at Grado, before the year 580. This instrument has been minutely described as having been two feet long by six inches deep, and as possessing thirty pipes, acted upon by fifteen keys or slides. It is very doubtful if they were familiar to the Romans, although an epigram of Julian the Apostate alludes to them. It seems, however, to be tolerably authenticated that one was sent by Constantine, in 766, as a present to Pepin, King of France. Improvements in their construction are attributed to Pope Sylvester, who died in 1003. When we reach the time of Chaucer, their use must have been common, for he speaks in his "Nonnes Priestes Tale" (None Priests Tale) of a crowing cock, "heighte chaunticlere."

> "His voic was merrier than the mery orgon
> On mass daies that in the chirches gon."

A somewhat curious record is made by another author which deserves quotation. Elfeg, Bishop of Winchester, procured an organ for his cathedral in 951, which was the largest then known, having twenty-six pairs of bellows, requiring seventy men to fill it with wind.

It is not needful to enter into details here, with regard to the slow and painful steps by which one obstacle after another was overcome. The poor bellows-treader, who passed his time playing leap-frog from one bellows to the other, has, in most cases, given place to the blower at the pump-handle or some mechanical appliance of power. There was a time when men for fingers used their clenched fists as though playing on the old carillon; for the spring of the key on an organ manual was, for lack of mechanical appliances, less susceptible to pressure than the keys on the pedal-board are now. As to the pedal-board itself, we must remember that while an organ is not regarded as an organ without it, and while there is little organ music written which can be played without pedals, the pedal-board is a comparatively recent addition.

It is a remarkable fact, and no less remarkable than significant, that with the organ with its polyphonic capacity, came in ever broadening circles the knowledge of the laws which govern music itself. Then ten fingers can do much, but they can only reach so far; when, however, the pedal key-board was added it became possible not only to multiply voices, but to carry each part distinctly, no matter what their compass. As long as the organ was in a rudimentary state, the rules which govern harmony were arbitrary and hypothetical; but as has already been stated, the growth of harmony was synchronous with the growth of the organ; and while this cannot be directly traced to the immediate influence of the organ, it should exercise due weight with musicians, and lays claim to their lasting gratitude.

Another great and important addition was yet to be made, and the one which to-day to the listener is perhaps the most marked feature of organ music. While the pedals enabled the organist to render each voice to the full extent of its capacity, it was long before what is commonly known as the sub-bass was added to them, thus making it possible to distinguish the pedal part from the manual, besides conferring upon the bass that breadth and volume which is so essential as a foundation to every musical composition.

Gradually the pedal-board was enlarged until, in some instruments, it reaches the dimensions of two octaves and a half; that is, from the C to the G, two octaves above. But the use of large pedal-boards has been of slow growth, and both in England and America it is common to find them with an octave and a fifth, or even with one octave. This is part of the grandfather before alluded to; but having in his day and generation done good service, he should be laid to rest with his forefathers. In order to play organ music a pedal-board must have at least two octaves. If anything, the upper octave is more important than the lower, and no organist can be at home on a board of less capacity. If I have dwelt at length on the value of the pedal-board it was because its importance justified it. Take it away and you might as well take away the organ itself.

To the organ there has been added stops of every possible nature; some of them peculiar to it, but most of them either resembling, or attempting to resemble, some instrument. Most stops give but one tone to

each key when pressed, but there are mixture stops having four ranks of pipes, which, when drawn, yield four
tones to each key. We have mechanical combinations
for drawing and *with*drawing whole rows of stops, and
combinations for drawing a whole organ at once. Instead of one, we have four organs, three for the hands,
and one for the feet. For one stop for the pedals we
have twenty. Couplers which connect one manual with
another, or each manual separately with the pedals, or
combine all four at once in an overwhelming flood of
sounds. A whole orchestra cannot surpass the tone-
power of the full organ, and no orchestra can be reduced to a more perfect pianissimo ; nor does the wonder cease here—steam and electricity have been called
in to supplement and manipulate what was already the
wonder of the age. What does it matter to the organist that his instrument requires five or six horse-power
to run it ? The seventy men can all stay at home now
and need not work the bellows, as in the days of good
Elfeg, Bishop of Winchester. Way back where nobody
can hear him there is a little monster puffing away, and
he says : "I am worth all that seventy men do, and a
good deal more besides, for I never get tired, and I can
make the organ hold out just as long as the gentleman at the key-boards." What is it to the organist
that only a part of his organ is before him and the remainder scattered around the church ? for does not the
lightning aid him in the chancel, in the crypt, so far
that the echoes just reach his ear ? His fingers guide
the electric current on its mission—the song of prayer
and praise. Fire and thunder, wind and water, all combine to do his bidding. Just as in the tempest, the

lightning of the electric fluid is followed by the pealing thunder of the double diapason. The power which turns the looms of half the world, which has carried civilization beyond the Rocky Mountains, and bears in safety across the fathomless sea the proudest navies that have ever floated into port, comes, after its week-day labor, to the Sabbath temple and there pours out its wealth of worship through the organ's ten thousand throats. Solemn, majestic, overwhelming! Too stupendous for conception, too full of adoration for thought to grasp or language frame.

But one says, "What! will you worship by machinery?" My friend, it is not the matter of how you shall worship which troubles you. Oh, no! I know plenty of men just like you. You are counting the cost of keeping up the batteries, of paying the organ tuner. You think that that engine burns too much fuel; you think they pay the organist too much. But let me tell you one thing: it is better that you should pay a machine to sing well for you than to provoke the ridicule of your neighbors by your unnatural grimaces, and your still more uncouth and unnatural attempts to vocalize. But this is a digression into which I have been inadvertently led. Before leaving the subject of the organ to take up that of the organist, in order to convey an adequate idea of the vastness of the complete organ to those who are not familiar with such matters, I wish to present a few details with regard to some of the greatest organs of Europe, which must convey to every one some idea of their dimensions. In the Benedictine Monastery at Weingarten is an organ of four rows of keys and sixty stops, fifteen of which are for

5

the fifth organ or pedal-board.   There are 6666 pipes in
this organ.   In the great organ there is a stop called
mixture, with twenty ranks of pipes.   The longest pipe
of this organ is thirty-two feet.   .

The organ in the Church of St. Peter and Paul contains 32 stops and 3270 pipes.   The pedal organ contains 20 stops.   In the choir organ there is a stop
called carillons, a set of small bells.   The organ in the
Cathedral of Freyburg has 68 stops, and is world-
famed not only for its power, but its Vox Humana.
The organ of Haarlem is 108 feet in height, 50 in
breadth, and has 68 stops.   The largest metal pipe is
32 feet long.   In some foreign instruments two sets of
pedals are provided, which may be described as great
and choir pedals.   The great pedal is in the usual
position ; the choir pedal is in front of the other, and
sloping.   It is so placed that the feet rest on it
naturally when stretched out in front of the performer.   There is a choir pedal of this kind in the
organ in the Minster at Ulm, built by Walcher, of
Ludwigsburg.   It is a very large instrument, having
100 sounding-stops.

While all these organs are phenomenally great, they
are also, with one or two exceptions, more than a
century old.   But it is to be questioned if the builders
of those great tone-castles did not, after all, succeed in
putting a better and purer tone into their instruments
than the builders of later days.   There is yet another
thing to be borne in mind, and that is that if all the
elements of nature were to combine with the organ
they would, after all, be only accessories.   Magnificent
as is the effect of external appliances, it must never be

forgotten that it is not them but the organ, and it alone. Beautiful, vast and various as are the combinations of stops, it must not be overlooked that the majority of them are ephemeral, superficial and dependent on the few foundation stops, such as the diapason and principal, for nearly every substantial effect. If the variety of stops were less and their caliber greater, in my opinion the organ would be a far more religious and effective instrument. Where the superficial stops are used without judgment the effect on the cultivated ear is grating and unpleasant to the last degree. These stops are nauseating from their very sweetness. An organist often has a hobby about a stop or a combination, and on Sunday morning he will go into the choir gallery and there put on some pet reed, with, perhaps, the tremolo, and smack his lips over it and grind away as though neither he nor the congregation had ever tasted sugar candy before.

It would be impossible to lay down any general rule for organ registration which did not admit of a thousand exceptions. If the amateur adheres to the unison stops he will generally be correct. If the organ is too small to admit of his using the intended registration, then he should be so acquainted with the nature of the stops indicated as to be able to in a manner substitute them. While all the registers and accessories to an organ which have been mentioned are to be desired, there are but few pieces which cannot be rendered on two manuals and a pedal-board of two octaves. These are absolutely indispensable, and it is as idle to try to play music on one manual, as it is to try to play pedals on an octave and a fifth. Referring to this latter, I will state that common as the grandfather pedal-board is, there has never yet been found any composer of classic organ music who has written any work which does not do most of the pedalling on the upper octave. With regard to stops, every builder outside of certain regulation registers makes his own specification, but to the student of the organ I would give one piece of advice: unless you are a pianist, don't go to the *organ*. If you are, learn to use the pedals with both feet, and with as much dexterity as you do your hands on the manuals; and when you accomplish that, stop-changing will come to you easily enough. Guard against defects not serious in themselves, and yet enough so to make them amusing; such as pressing down the pedal one or two seconds before beginning a piece, or slowing up on an Amen until the choir either break down or sound like bagpipes. These are a few of the eccentricities of the amateur organist which should be avoided, and so the best guard is this: don't play anything that is not written; don't retard when it is not intended; don't accelerate the verse of a hymn, because it commences with the words, "Oh, hasten; come, hasten." This may be descriptive music, but I have not found it catalogued anywhere. Schumann said, "Neglect no opportunity of practising on the organ. There is no other instrument which inflicts such prompt chastisement on offensive and defective composition or execution." As to the character of organ music, let us see what Schneider, one of the most thorough of organists, has to say: "Beautiful, simple melodies, calming the heart, floating on powerful, solemn and thrilling harmonies—these are the first fundamental elements of which alone all organ playing ought to be composed; ornaments and graces cannot but appear as a desecration of what is holy, as a stain on what is beautiful and venerable. It is as a disfiguration of what is in the first place absolutely necessary: that a good organist should have a complete knowledge of theory, since the instrument requires always full, complete harmony."

The fugue is the best species of music an organist can employ, provided his subject be lofty and sublime, which it can only be by deviating from everything that is trivial, secular or common. Happily the musical world is enriched by many masterly fugues, composed expressly for the organ; and no player need deprecate the charge of unskilfulness who has modesty sufficient to prefer the works of Handel, Graun, Bach, Altorchstberger and others to his own extemporaneous effusion. The introductory is supposed to have a character of its own. It should be in grave and solemn style, abounding in full, close-wrought harmony, and inspiring a feeling of reverential awe. The concluding or out-voluntary is that in which the organist generally shows off the full power and effects of the instrument he presides over. The pieces best suited for this occasion are those expressly composed for the organ, consisting generally of an introduction and fugue wherein the pedals may be employed.

Dr. Stainer says: "A good organist may be known, if by nothing else, by his use of the crescendo of the swell organ. A bad player, when he has a leg to spare seems to think it cannot be better employed than pumping the swell-pedal up and down, with utter disregard to the composer's intentions. It might often be said that such performers try to use the swell-pedal even when one leg cannot be spared, and thus frequently sacrifice beautiful pedal passages by consigning their rendering to the frantic efforts of the left foot only." The Encyclopædia Britannica says: "The essence of legitimate playing is putting the feet over each other freely, so as to use the alternate method as much as possible." Rink, in his voluminous works, has left his lasting tribute of reverence for the monarch of instruments.

It would be impossible, if not useless, further to quote authorities on this subject, yet there is one work to which I must allude. It is Ritter's great "Organ School," in three volumes, translated by John Paul Morgan. I trust that in this place it may not be inappropriate that I should pay my tribute of affectionate respect to one who, throughout his all too brief life, was so loved and respected by all who knew him. While I do not in the least overrate the value of Ritter's vast compilation, I am well aware that I am influenced largely by the fact that it was translated by my teacher. And now, for the benefit of the one-legged organists who stamp round the pedals on Sunday, while their fingers perform the vilest sacrilege, let me record this fact: I never heard him improvise. Great as his knowledge of the doctrine of music must have been by reason of his being the translator of Richter's "Manual of Harmony," his "Manual on Counterpoint," and Richter's treatise on the fugue, and notwithstanding the fact that he wrote and published a large amount of music, I must repeat, I never knew him to be guilty of the impertinence of improvising. It is now seven years since we followed him to the grave, but his words are ever with me. This he said : "Under God I have been the instrument of translating the noblest work that was ever written for the organ." If, instead of writing on the walls of the church, " Holiness becometh thine house, O Lord," that text were tattooed on the organist, it might be more respected.

John Paul Morgan was an ideal organist. His instrument to him was as sacred as the building in which it was placed, and his reverence for it was such that nothing could have induced him to play on it anything frivolous or secular. Conscience, conscience, conscience ! Bishops, priests and deacons have to feel a call to enter into the service of the sanctuary. Is the organist nothing more than a hireling? How is it possible that persons believing in the religion which they hear preached daily, can go to their organ and in act, if not in word, let it be understood that any kind of music is good enough for God. The world is full of good, beautiful organ music ; how is it that you do in church what you dare not do in your own parlor? You can be as sacrilegious with an organ as you can be with your lips.

The most unpleasant feature of the so-called improvising is that the improvisator has, in the course of his or her life, actually strung together some musical progressions, and that each time that he seats himself at the organ, it is to grind out the same composition, Sunday after Sunday and year after year. There are very few people who know aught of harmony, and there are still fewer who, knowing, have the gift to make

a practical use of it.   It is better not to play at all
than to play badly.   Many times I have been asked
the question: " How long will it take me to learn the
organ? "   And when I have said that a couple of years
might make them organists, I have been met with the
reply that " —— learned to play in three months."   I
do not discuss the fact, but retire from the field in as
good order as I can.   Nobody ever did learn to play
the organ in three or six months, or in a year.   That is
one proposition, and another is, that nobody ever *will*.
Organ playing doesn't mean just playing hymn tunes,
but it means playing Bach and Handel.   It means
deserving your own approbation: It means power, not
only over your instrument, but over the people who
listen to you.   It means that you are above the ·igno-
rant and *that* because your labor has entitled you to
be.

Show me a good organist and I will show you a fine
brain.   Show me one of your slop-shop organists and
I will show one who neither fears God nor regards
man.   The highest happiness that a man can have is
an approving conscience.   The criticism of one musician is worth more than a whole city full of ignorant
eulogists.   Don't be satisfied with being a half-way
musician.   To be thorough one must practise every
day, and this not for the time that they are learning,
but for all time.   Said Federlein: " Without struggle
there is no victory; without labor, no success."

CHAPTER VIII.

OUTLINE OF THE ORGAN.

A MANUAL is a key-board. The pedal-board is a small manual for the feet with raised keys to correspond to the black keys on the manuals.

Stops.—All stops are registers, but all registers are not stops. Every stop represents an instrument and should properly run the whole length of the manual, although one or two, sometimes more, treble stops reach only as low as F, the fourth line in the bass clef, where they are continued by one bass stop. Pipes are sometimes of metal and sometimes of wood. This is for the reason that as wood and metal produce different qualities of tone, the color-sound of each stop depends on the material of which it is made. As every complete stop on the manual includes sixty pipes, it is easy to see how the multiplication of stops increases the cost of the organ.

The pipes of an organ range in all degrees of length from thirty-two feet down to three-eighths of an inch. Organ builders classify these under the head of thirty-two, sixteen, eight, four, and two-foot tones. As the pedal-board has but two octaves, and the key-board but five, the whole number of keys does not exceed the scale of a seven-octave piano. The unison, or eight-foot tone, is that which corresponds in pitch to the treble and bass clefs. These are always the most powerful stops on the manuals, and of them the diapason is always the greatest. The four-foot tone includes all stops which give the octave above the eight-foot tone, and is to the organist what 8va is to the pianist. Of these there are also a number; most important of which is the Principal. The two-foot tone is that which gives the tone two octaves above the one written, thus enabling the organist to strike two octaves with one finger. Of the two-foot stops, the fifteenth is the most common. It is so called because it gives the fifteenth tone in the scale above the eight-foot tone. Even now the octave capacity of one key has not been fully stated, for if we have climbed *up* so many octaves, why should we not descend, thus enabling *one finger* on the organ to do what *both hands* cannot accomplish on the piano-forte. The sub-octave is called the Bourdon, and illustrates a remarkable principle in acoustics; for while the Bourdon is only an eight-foot pipe, it gives a sixteen-foot tone. I am not aware to whom we are indebted for this discovery, but the principle, like most laws, is simple enough after being known. And this leads me to speak of organ pipes in general.

Pipes.—If a four-foot pipe be, as is customary, open at the top, it produces a four-foot tone. Closed at the top, the same pipe makes an eight-foot tone; that is, a tone an octave below. The column of air which enters the pipe at its base traverses its length twice, that is, eight feet; whereas, were the stopper removed, it would only travel four feet. Thus an eight-foot Bourdon is made to give as deep a tone as a sixteen-foot Diapason, but not as powerful; and a sixteen-foot as deep as a thirty-two foot Diapason. Many names are given to stops, but they can all be classified under a few heads—pipes stopped or open; or else, metal, wooden or reeds. Schneider says: "Organ pipes may be distributed into flue-pipes and reed-pipes. They are made either of metal or wood. The form of the metal pipes is either that of a cylinder, or of a cone, direct or inverted. The form of the wooden pipes is generally that of a rectangular prism, though occasionally they are also pyramidal, these being the forms most easily constructed, and most advantageous as to tone. Pipes are either altogether open at the top, or they are stopped totally or partially; the wooden pipes in the former case by means of a stopper, and the metal pipes by a cap. Some of the stopped pipes have a small tube passing through the centre of the cap or stopper; this is called a chimney; these of course are only partially stopped." Another feature of the organ which has no counterpart in any instrument or instruments is the high-pitched stops, which are included under the head of mixture stops. It is an anomaly without a parallel. Any stop is called mixture which produces more than one tone at the pressure of one key. Even some are so included, as the twelfth and seventeenth or tierce, and this because, as they are never used alone, they form harmonic combinations foreign to any pure system of harmony. For example, if one mixture stop has three ranks, each key will give the common triad. If the key C be struck, the result will be the common chord of C; but if to this be added another key, the third, E, a second triad is now sounded, and this in discord with the first. Add then the remainder of the dominant seventh, and in like manner we have two more triads, making a discord which must be heard to be appreciated. We have the chords of C, E, G, B flat, complete. This makes twelve tones; even the reading of it is distressing. The triad of C is C, E, G. That of E is E, G sharp, B. The chord of G is G, B, D. And that of B flat, B flat, D, F. I have written of this at an unintentional length, but as it is not easy to make clear, and is but little known to many, I have been thus minute in the attempt. But before leaving this set of stops, I must answer the question which has naturally arisen : Why are they used at all? They are for use only with heavy eight and four-foot tones, that the pure harmonies may be so powerful as to cover up the discords, and cause them, while not obtrusive, to still impart a crash and brilliancy to the full organ which can be had in no other manner.

Reeds.—The coloring capacity of the reed-stops is perhaps more varied than all others ; but this very high coloring renders it dangerous, for there is no coloring so high as not to become common by constant use. Some of these reed-stops are most plaintive, and form a marked contrast to the martial character of others. The reed differs from other stops in its construction, in that tone is produced by the current of air vibrating a little tongue of metal, thus producing the peculiar quality. This makes itself felt over the most powerful organ, and for tenderness or force cannot be overrated. But while no organ is complete without reeds, it should be remembered that unless they are tuned at least once a month they were best left out altogether, for one reed requires more care than twelve other stops. The slightest variation of temperature, the jarring of the organ by the pumper, the vibrations of the reed-tongue itself, dust, moisture, all these things affect it, and that to such a degree as to render it in a few weeks quite unfit for use. Here the old rule, which knows no exception, applies : If you would have a good thing, you must pay for it. Some of the reed stops are Trumpet, Clarion, or octave-trumpet, Bassoon, Vox Humana, Hautboy, etc., etc. And now as to the possible future of the organ. This is dependent on three agencies. The first, because it recognizes tone ; the second, because it causes tone ; and the third, because on it both of the preceding are dependent. These three are the ear, the science of acoustics, and the application of mechanics. In the field of speculation it is a recognized tenet that we may be surrounded by forces as active and influential as those of either light or sound, but having no senses through which they may reach us their action is not directly recognized, and their origin unknown. This is a glimpse into a field into which, at some future day, I hope to enter more fully, but it has been brought under consideration by the reflection that as without the ear the organ would have never existed, without the continuance of the ear it would immediately cease to exist. The ear has shown itself capable of as great cultivation as the eye, as may be easily demonstrated by the study of the history of music.

"Mr. Ruskin, in a most interesting passage in 'Modern Painters,' shows that the sense of color has been developed in the course of ages. He says the Greek

sense of color seems to have been so comparatively
dim and uncertain that it is almost impossible to ascer-
tain what the real idea was which they attached to any
word alluding to hue," (" Color Music," by Rev. J.
Crofts). Every harmony which some more progressive
ear discovered had to fight its way to the comprehension of all the other ears. Thus it is that it has been
evolutionized from the apprehension of the old Greek
modes up to the polyphony and superlative orchestration of Baireuth. It will readily be perceived that the
effect has been placed before the *cause*, the ear before
acoustics, because without the sensation of sound,
sound itself could not be taken into consideration directly *as* sound. The organ had a scale ranging from
nine to ten octaves. It does not seem probable that
this limit will soon, if ever, be exceeded successfully ;
for as we increase the dimensions of pipes, we diminish
the number of vibrations in inverse ratio, and conversely
with the diminution of a pipe. As all sound is the result of vibration, it follows that if vibration be too in-
frequent, it becomes little more than a succession of
puffs, like those of a railroad engine. On the other
hand, if it be so frequent as to create, instead of a succession of waves, a constant current of air, the sound
becomes too attenuated and loses the power of creating
either sensation or color. There must be sixteen vibrations in a second to produce the lowest tone, while
the upper limit of sound is produced by 38,000 vibrations in a second. So much for the vibrations of the
extremes. What has been, shall be again. The
growth that has taken place in the nature and construction of organ-pipes must continue until the science

of acoustics has yielded up the key of her every hidden
chamber. The organ is already the most elaborate
complexity of mechanism ever applied to musical purposes, but it is either in its childhood, or else must always remain a most imperfect instrument. This may
seem rather at variance with all that has been said,
but I hope to make this clear without seeming inconsistent. In a chorus, or in an orchestra, where increase or decrease of volume is required, it is accomplished by all the voices or instruments growing louder
through additional pressure of either wind or hand,
and the reverse by diminishing the pressure. The difference between a stop and a voice is that the stop can
never be any louder or softer, but that the tone of the
organ can only be increased or diminished by the addition or subtraction of the stops. The effect is never
the same as that of an orchestra, or a chorus, for *they* increase and diminish altogether, where such effects are
required, thereby preserving the same quality of tone,
which can never be the case in an organ. True, you
may make it so soft as to be scarcely audible, but that
will probably be only one stop, and when the full organ is used as the climax it will have been by the addition of stops, and such cannot be legitimately considered a crescendo. The swell organ answers every
requirement so far as it goes, but as it is the smallest
of the three organs it serves rather to show off the im-
perfections of the other two. It is very easy to suggest
and advise the impossible, but I should regret to be
thought ignorant of the defects as well as the merits of
the instrument. If, instead of having only one organ
in a swell, each one, not excepting the pedal-organ,

were placed in swell-boxes, the effect of the crescendo
of the whole instrument would indeed be overwhelming
in the extreme. There may be other ways by which
such a result might be accomplished, but none have
ever suggested themselves to me. There are doubtless
many other mechanical improvements, but I cannot believe that any of them is second in importance to this.
I should not wish, as so lengthy a sketch would imply,
to seem to run the organ as a hobby, or even to say
that it is capable of superseding any other single instrument. Its future does not lie in superseding others,
but in developing *itself.* The factors to which it is indebted for being will not forsake it on the threshold
of its greatness. Having now considered the past,
present, and possible future of the organ, there remains but one more subject demanding attention.

The position of the organ.—If we have a picture, we
hang it where it catches the best light. If we have
a flower, we so locate it that its perfume may most
readily reach us ; but with the organ this rule seems
to be reversed. In the small town where I live
there are four two-manual organs. Of these, three
are so placed that more than half their power is
lost. The absurdity of purchasing a three thousand
dollar instrument in order to place it where it can
give but one thousand dollars' worth of tone is too
manifest to require comment. In order that an organ shall speak it must be so placed that there will
be no impediment to its tone. The long pipes should
never be where the ceiling is so low that they must be
thrust through it. The instrument itself should never
be located in a corner or recess of any kind. As sound

has a tendency to ascend, it is always to be desired
that an organ should be placed as nearly on a level
with the congregation as possible. Every practical organist should be familiar with the structure of his
organ-pipes. Not only to enable him to rectify in case
of need, but that he may, by his knowledge of the
character of each stop, be better able to judge of its
possible effect on others, sitting at a distance. The
name register is given to every draw-stop and coupler.
It also includes whatever else there may be, such as
bellows-signal, bellows-check, tremolo, etc. So when
we consider the *verb* to register a piece, its meaning
will be readily understood.

The swell organ is an organ varying in size in different instruments, and entirely separate from the main
organ. It is shut up in a box which has a number of
little doors in its front connected by a lever with what
is called the swell-pedal, which in its turn is operated
by the right foot. The effect of the crescendo on
opening the doors is beautiful in the extreme; that is,
of course, where the intention of the composer is followed. It is not my purpose in this place to speak of
the internal arrangement of the organ; that is, the construction of the bellows, or sets of bellows, of the wind-
chests, slides, pallets, conductors, and so on, for no one
can understand these things by description alone, but
must have an opportunity of seeing for themselves their
practical application.

Tuning.—If the question has presented itself before, why should we get fine organs if they are to
be played on by people who don't understand how
to play them, the same question should present itself

6

as to keeping them in tune.   The finer an organ
is, the worse it is for being out of tune.   Where it
is possible, it is cheaper to employ a tuner for the
organ by the year, as the piano tuners are engaged,
than to suddenly be aroused to the fact that through
neglect and carelessness the instrument is in a horrible condition.   If not this, then an organ ought to be
overhauled entirely once a year, and the reed-stops
should be tuned once a month.   It is the misfortune of
the organ that, being the property of a number of people, it is to no one person's interest to look after it,
while the piano, being the property of an individual, is
studiously cared for.   It is to be regretted that church
people, while so particular as to the condition of their
own instruments, do not care whether the instrument of
the Lord is in order or not.   I trust that no one will
think that this is said with any feeling of disrespect
either to creed or congregation; but looking at it from
another point of view, it is certainly inconsistent that
instruments costing many thousands of dollars should
not receive as much care as those costing a few hundreds.   In this sketch of the organ, it was my wish to
make clear to the public in general some parts of that
noblest of instruments, thereby enabling them to form
a conception of the complexity of its structure, the di-
versity of its tone-qualities, the intricate nature of its
manipulation, requiring of the feet that they should
play on the pedal-board while they, at the same time,
make a judicious use of the swell and combination
pedals; of the hands that shall manage two, three, and
even four manuals, draw and withdraw registers and
turn music, while the eyes take cognizance of every-

thing, but more particularly of the music being read. Trusting that I have intelligibly acquitted myself in these respects, I wish, before closing, once more to re-iterate that the organ deserves good treatment at the hands both of players and tuners; and it is with the earnest hope of conveying such a conviction to at least a few that this paper has been written.

CHAPTER IX.

USE AND INFLUENCE OF BELLS.

EVERY piece of matter which, upon being struck, emits a sound may be regarded as an instrument of percussion; and the more sonorous the nature of the body so struck, the more perfectly is it adapted to that purpose. The variety and use of such instruments is great, but their relations, one to the other, are not always apparent, as, for example, we do not immediately classify under the same head drums and bones with such instruments as the bell or the piano, and yet a moment's thought makes their relationship manifest. In the case of all instruments, whether wind, string or percussion, the end sought is the same—vibration, but the means to that end vary with the character of each of these three classes of instruments. The weakest are the string, and the most far-reaching, the percussion: it therefore required no particular sagacity to recognize the latter as that best fitted for call and signal. Nor does the law of natural selection stop here, for of percussion instruments the largest and most vibratory were those best adapted for such purposes, and of these the drum and the bell were the most prominent and effective.

In the choice between these last two the prolonged and sustained vibrations of the bell gave to it a pre-

dominance in power and sweetness over all other instruments of a like nature. One of the most graceful
flowers that grows is the *moretous campannula*, the bell
flower, which in its simple grace was the mute foreshadowing of its silver-tongued prototype. In despite
of the sinister use to which the bell has been frequently
put, it may be considered with justice the emblem of
peace, as opposed to its rival percussion brother, the
drum, and like the olive branch, tells the story of
peace on earth. Drums perish with the war in which
they were beaten, but bells endure through peace and
war, forever perpetuating their own memory. If the
Church may be considered the bulwark of the State,
then the bell may rightfully be regarded as its official
utterance. It may be that in our pursuit of this subject we shall find that its position as a social factor has
been materially altered, but if the bell has been with-
drawn from active life, so far from losing, it has rather
acquired dignity. Indeed, in the history of bells we
find a striking analogy to the life of man, rewarded in
old age with the crown of honored years. It is therefore with a sense of profound veneration not unmixed
with awe that I approach the consideration of the
voice of the steeple and the invitation to prayer.
Whether we regard the bell as an historical, ecclesiastical, architectural or musical agency, it occupies a
prominence in the life of the past to which men of to-
day are slow in according recognition. While we must
regard it from all these separate points of view, they
are so interwoven as to be almost identical. If we
attempt to regard the bell from an historical standpoint, we are reminded that its first prominence in Eu-

rope was given to it by Christianity. If, however, we
regard it as an ecclesiastical institution, secular history
confronts us on every hand with the manifold uses of
the bell for purposes other than those of ecclesiasticism.
As the badge of the Christian was the cross, and of
the Mohammedan, the crescent, quite as sharp cut was
the line drawn between the Christian and Mohammedan call to prayer. Wherever the bell was heard there
was Christianity. So clearly was this recognized and
admitted that wherever the rule of the Turk extended,
there the voice of the bell was silent. Thus it was that
the cross and the bell went side by side, and with the
banishment of the one came the silence of the other.
Men grew to love and venerate their bells, and as this
feeling intensified, superstition and ignorance endowed
them with miraculous powers, and whether used in
cursing or blessing, the bell was an important factor.

The architectural influence of bells, while really very
great, has been of a negative character and cannot
therefore be considered independently. Bell music
might, from its peculiar character, be a subject afford-
ing separate consideration; but such a dissertation
could only interest the musician, and it is for the
perusal of the general reader that these pages are intended. As the effect of causes which have to a large
extent ceased to exist, the conclusion forces itself
upon us that the bell has passed its maximum influence,
and, though by slow degrees, is in the path of decadence and desuetude.

As an instrument of ecclesiasticisms the bell is what
it always was, but it has passed out of civil life, and as
an historical factor will never become prominent again.

The fact is, the bell is not in sympathy with the age; but with the Church it is different: it peals for the marriage and it tolls for the dead. Though far *above* the world it yet speaks *to* the world. It tells of kneeling congregations, of officiating priests, of the inspired organ, the chanting choir, incense, painting, sculpture. Of all these things it tells, and yet more, for it speaks of the hearts of the worshipping thousands. Morning, noon and evening its voice is heard, and through the silence of the night it marks the hours for the sleeping world. Like the choral, it is a chapter of memories, but with the outside world its place has been filled and must so continue.

The bell, in order to be heard at a distance, had to be elevated, and this compelled the erection of high towers. The higher the tower the farther went the sound, and with the growth of the tower all the other architectural proportions had to be modified to preserve that harmonious whole which Schlagel called "Frozen music in stone." But here also it is safe to say the limit has been reached, and attention is now turned more upon utility than the æsthetic, and the successors of the old bell-towers, like the old bells, will grow fewer and fewer as the spirit of the age develops itself. But admitting that this active architectural influence has come to an end, there yet remains the negative principle which will ever continue in effect.

Strange as it may at first seem, the daily paper is the bell's deadliest enemy, and in the rustle of its columns we hear folded all, and more than all, that was told by the bell of former days. For great public sig-

nals among ancient peoples the trumpet was in most
general use, but the sound of the bell was more far-
reaching than that of the trumpet, and by tacit consent
the latter passed into disuse; but the old order ever
changeth, and in the inarticulate utterance of the
newspaper, whose voice is heard so far as steam and
electricity can carry it, we can hear the doom of the
great bell as a servant of the public.   It has done its
work well and faithfully; but loving it, yes hallowing
it, as we may, we cannot help the feeling that it is a
part of the dead past, forming a component of a chapter over which has been written the word, Finis; part
of that chapter in which the Crusades occupy so important a place; part of that chapter in which feudalism and chivalry constituted the base and bulwark of
society.   Yes, the chapter is finished; but as we close
it with a sigh, the present reality supplants the memories of the past, and while we deplore the decadence of
the art of bell-ringing and the love of bells, we are compelled to realize the law of compensation as we relin-
quish our hold upon the usages of the past.

So it is not altogether with regret that we lay aside
the historical chapter on bells; for, viewing them from
our modern and utilitarian standpoint, they must be
regarded conditionally, and in our consideration of the
bell we must remember that it may become quite as
much of a curse as a blessing, and that where they do
not exist in perfection, their room is much to be pre-
ferred.   On a certain time, Bordeaux rose in rebellion,
and as a mark of humiliation her bells were taken
from her; when, however, the period of expiation had
passed and the bells were to be reinstated, the citizens

of that municipality declined to receive them back, alleging as their reason that they had enjoyed such rest and quiet in their absence that they wished that absence continued.

These things are matters, not only of taste but of habit; and while no sweeping denunciation of bells is here intended, it can be conclusively shown that bell-ringing can be productive of quite as much evil as it has ever done good. The action taken by some of our American cities in condemning bell-ringing sufficiently evidences the fact that the feeling against bells is growing. If, on the score of utility, it be urged that without the bell people would not know when to go to church, the answer readily presents itself : if churches ·need bells to call people to hours of regular worship, why should not the theatres stand in far greater need of them ? I have noticed that in the Jewish syna-gogues no bell is used, and yet the congregations meet with quite as much punctuality as those of the Christian churches. We do ring bells for fires because, as it is not customary to set the time at which a fire shall take place, this is the only means by which the public may be notified. If, however, the public use of bells be urged on account of their beautiful effect, then indeed we are confronted with an argument possessing great weight, but which, in order to be effective, re-quires other conditions than those to which the average American citizen is accustomed. The beauty of all bells is dependent upon their quality or purity of tone and their relative pitch. If these essentials have been supplied, the effect of one bell will, in most cases, ful-fil the object for which it was cast, viz., that of beauty and solemnity; but if the tone be either shrill or impure the effect is neither beautiful nor solemn. In using the term pitch I have been careful to qualify it as relative; and this for the reason that as all harmony is based on a system of relative tones, bells can form no exception to the laws of harmonic construction. It has been said that under certain conditions the effect of a bell is beautiful and solemn, but even where these conditions are present, that effect is largely dependent upon its location. These then are the three essentials to bell music,—purity, pitch and location.

The importance of placing bells in as lofty a position . as may be attained is better understood when we remember that it is to them that towers of any height owe their existence only as the home of the bell. Prior to the use of large bells, towers were unknown save for purposes of defence, but like the growth of harmony with the organ, the growth of the tower with the bell has been synchronous. The higher the tower the further will be heard the voice which it contains, and its tone be mellowed and softened in its immediate vicinity.

Archæologists have worried themselves mightily as to the age of bells, but as the birth of the large bell is of a comparatively recent date, the antiquity of the baby bells, from which no doubt the big ones have grown, is a matter of very little concern. They were in use in Egypt; the Jewish High-Priest used them on his robe; Egyptians, Jews, Greeks and Romans alike employed them in their temple services, and among the last-mentioned nation a secular use of the bell, such as to call people to an auction sale or a distribution of provisions, was common; but no matter whether in the temple service or in the public mart, only hand bells were in use, and the great bell of to-day had to wait the processes of evolution.

The case of the average American bell violates every one of the above-named conditions. They are swung low, are small, and pitched without reference one to another. It is cheaper to build low towers and to have small bells, but cheapness was never the road to the artistic. If, therefore, the bell be neither useful nor artistic why should this perpetual jangle of an hundred church bells grate on the quiet of the Sunday morning—noon and night. In Holland, Belgium, Italy and France, where the artistic is always kept in view, they have bells; but such glorious bells! Of these, their dimension and number, I shall speak later. At present the utility and history of the bell must engage our attention.

This instrument of percussion, as has been before intimated, has played a most important part in the history of architecture, especially ecclesiastical architecture, and it would be difficult to consider the one without a brief mention of the other. If the bell built the tower, the tower cast the bell. The higher the tower the further would the bell be heard, and as the towers grew in height they grew proportionately massive, and the idea was not long in presenting itself of a bell to suit the tower, as well as a tower to suit the bell, for the ever increasing strength of the one warranted a proportionate increase in the weight of the other.

" The introduction of bells is attributed to Paulinus, Bishop of Nola, in Campania, about the year 400, but there is an epistle of that bishop still extant in which he describes his church, but makes no mention of either tower or bell, yet it is not a little remarkable that the general name for bell was nolæ or campanæ, and hence the word noll, as meaning the sound of a single bell, and campanile, a bell tower. Sabianus, who was pope in 604, ordered the bells to ring the *horæ canonicæ* at the proper times during the day. And Berendic, Abbot of Wearmouth, brought his bells from Italy about the year 680. Bells were hung in towers in the East in the ninth, and in Germany in the eleventh century. Those that were in use before are supposed to be hand bells; several examples as old as the sixth century are still preserved in some parts of Europe and the United Kingdom. St. Patrick's bells, St. Ninian's bell, St. Gall's bell and others are plates of iron riveted together. St. Gall's bell, about 646, is still shown in the monastery of the city called by his name in Switzerland. In the thirteenth century, larger bells were cast, but it was not until the end of the fifteenth century that they began to assume greater proportions."

In the councils of Cologne it is said, "Let bells be blessed, as the trumpets of the church militant, by which the people are assembled to hear the word of God; the clergy to announce His mercy by day, and His truth in their nocturnal vigils; that by their sound the faithful may be invited to prayers, and that the spirit of devotion in them may be increased. The Fathers have also maintained that the demons, affrighted by the sound of bells calling Christians to prayer, would flee away, and when they fled, the persons of the faithful would be secure ; that the destructions of lightnings, of whirlwinds would be averted, and the spirits of the storm defeated." The far-reaching, almost omnipresent sound of the bell impressed men powerfully, and, after all, it was *not* so singular that with their reverence for their bells there should have grown up a superstition which overshadowed their feelings of reverence. Even in early history, when there existed none but bells of the smallest character, the sense of safety and protection from evil through their use is marked and general. As the Christian era advanced, and bells grew both in size and dignity, their offices were multiplied and their virtues augmented. No matter of what material it was composed, the bell was a sacred instrument, and its powers were invoked on all occasions. The explanation is simpler than may at first appear, for the bell was the one remedy for the one evil, and that evil appearing in every conceivable and inconceivable form, on the land and on the sea, on the mountain and in the valley, at home or abroad, in the air, nay, in the sanctuary itself, was the spirit of darkness in the form of demons. When the storm lashed the sea into a froth of fury, and the great ships danced upon the billows and were hurled upon the rocks, then was the demon power at its height, and then it was that the rebuking and exorcising power of the bell was called into play, and the demons after an ineffectual resistance, fled from the scene of their discomfiture. Thus in times of earthquake, eclipse of the sun and moon, and other unusual phenomena, the bell was a constant source of comfort and a sure defence against the powers of darkness. But even here the bell did not reach the maximum of its potency. Having followed a man through all his career with its benign influence, it exercised that influence in its most signal capacity in the closing moments of his life. It is in the hour of dissolution, when the body and mind are alike enfeebled and benumbed, that the whole power of the demon world is gathered and concentrated upon the effort to capture and destroy the departing spirit. Then it was amid the agonies of dissolution that the bell was wont to be sounded, and the poor soul was comforted and solaced in his warfare with the demon host, and the devils trembled and fled as the consecrated sound reached their ears, and the spirit rested from its labors.*

The use of bells which called worshippers together is supposed to be of Christian origin, but it is said that the feast of Osiris in Egypt was announced by the ringing of bells. In speaking of the image supposed to have belonged to St. Patrick himself, Kingsley says, "Where, too, hung till late years (it is now preserved in Dublin) an ancient bell; such a strange little oblong bell such as the Irish saints carry with them to keep off demons; one of those magic bells which appear, so far as I am aware, in no country save Ireland and Scotland till we come to Tartary and the Buddhists; such a bell as came down from heaven to St. Senan; such a bell as St. Fursey sent flying through the air to greet St. Cuandu at his devotions when he could not come himself; such a bell as another saint, wandering

---

* Putnam's "Dictionary of Dates" says, "Bells were used in churches by order of Pope John IX., as a defence, by ringing them against thunder and lightning, about 900."

in the woods, rang till a stag came out of the covert, and carried it for him on his horns."

If bells have exercised so large an influence in the cause of religion, they have also been the prelude of some of the darkest and most sinister chapters in modern history. As in the case of the "Holy Ghost" bell in the tower at Strasbourg, only rung when two fires are seen in the town at once; or that other, the "Recall" bell, only rung at the approach of storms; or, as in the time of Charles. VII., of France, to call in the cattle at the approach of the English yeomanry; or, as when the Florentines, in answer to the threat of Charles VIII. that if his demands were not acceded to he would blow his trumpets, replied, "And we will ring our bells;" or as during the fair at Leyden, the bell of St. Panchrist rang out on the night to tell the multitude gathered there that the enemy was at the gates, and that their only alternative was flight or famine in the walls of the beleaguered city; or as on that Easter Monday, when at the ringing of the vesper bell all Sicily rose as a man, and eight thousand French, without distinction of age or sex, were massacred by the enraged populace; or as on that never-to-be-forgotten night, when the bell of the Luxerrois rang the funeral knell of from thirty to seventy thousand Huguenots.

It is curious to read many of the bell inscriptions, having in them a ring both of quaintness and simplicity. For example, the bell in St. Paul's Cathedral has this inscription: "Richard Phelps made me, 1716." Another in the Westminster Abbey tower: "Remember John Whitmell, Isabelle his wife, and William Rus,

who first gave this bell, 1430. New cast July, 1599,
and in April, 1738. Richard Phelps, T. Lester, fecit."
The oldest bell, somewhat smaller, dates from 1583.
The next oldest is the second largest bell, date 1598.
It bears an inscription, "Timpanis patrem laudate so-
nantibus altum. Gabriel Goodman, decanus 1598."
Another bell :—

> "Thomas Lester, London, made me,
>   And with the rest I will agree,
>   Seventeen hundred and forty three."

One of the Ghent bells bears an inscription not un-
common in Flanders in the low countries :

> "My name is Roland,
>   When I tole then it is for a fire;
>   When I chime, then there is stormy weather in Flanders."

Upon the famous Holy Ghost bell in Strasbourg
tower is dated, " 1375, 3 nonas Augusti," weighs about
eight tons, and, "O Rex gloriæ Christe veni cum
pace." These inscriptions are all taken from Mr.
Harweis' book entitled, "Music and Morals." Two
more inscriptions I will give from two old English
bells, " Hac nova campana Margaretta est nominata ; "
and the other in the same place, " In mustis annis
resonet campana Johannis." On the subject of bell
music I prefer to quote again from Mr. Harweis : "To
Belgium belongs the honor of having first understood
and felt bells as musical tones, and devised that aërial
and colossal musical instrument known as the carillon.

" The rise of bell music in Belgium was sudden and
rapid. In the sixteenth century the use of several
bells in connection with the town-clocks was common

enough. Even little tunes were played at the quarters and half hours. The addition of a second octave was clearly only a matter of time. In the seventeenth century carillons were found in all the principal towns of Belgium, and between the seventeenth and eighteenth centuries all the finest carillons now in use, including those of Mechlin, Antwerpt Bruges, Ghent and Louvain, were set up. There seems to have been no limit to the number of bells, except the space and strength of the building. Antwerpt Cathedral has sixty-five bells; St. Rombaud, Mechlin, forty-four bells; Bruges, forty bells and one Bourdon, or heavy bass bell; Ghent, thirty-nine; Tournay, forty; St. Gertrude, at Louvain, forty."

These colossal instruments, as they have been correctly termed, possess in a remarkable degree that element of sympathy so powerful and effective as to be universally acknowledged. The conductor wielding his baton, or the organist at his instrument, influences a greater number of people distributed through a larger space than by any other ordinary musical agency; but with the carillon, the incidental essentials to such a great hearing no longer exist. Outside the walls of the cathedral or the concert hall the strains of music reach us but faintly, and the more *piano* passages are altogether lost; but with the carillon the conditions are reversed. Where we formerly required a roof and walls, as it were, to draw the sound closer and retain it in its entirety, with this great, free flood of bell music we want heaven for our organ loft, and the whole earth for the audience chamber.

Bells were, and are, in the Catholic Church conse-

7

crated, the bishop performing the ceremony.   He
made five crosses pronouncing these words: " Santi-
ficetur et consecretur domine, signum istud in nomine
patris et filii et spiritus sancti.   In honorem sancti N.
pax tibi."

A singular and sinister usage of the bell existed in
former times, and I shall quote the passage alluding to
it without change or curtailment.   The excommunication of bell, book and candle is a solemnity belonging
to the Church of Rome.   The officiating minister pro-
nounces the formula of excommunication, consisting of
maledictions on the head of the person anathematized,
and closes the pronouncing of the sentence by shutting
the book from which it is read, taking a lighted candle
and casting it to the ground, and tolling the bell as for
the dead.   This mode of excommunication appears to
have existed in the Western churches as early as the
eighth century.   Its symbolism may be explained by
quoting two or three sentences from the conclusion of
the form of excommunication used in the Scottish
Church before the Reformation: " Cursed be they from
the crown of the head to the sole of the foot.   Out be
they taken from the book of life.   And as this candle
is cast from the sight of men, so be their souls cast
from the sight of God into the deepest pit of hell."
The Rubric adds, "And the candle being dashed on
the ground and quenched, let the bell be rung."   So
also the sentence of excommunication against the mur-
derers of the Archbishop of Dublin in 1534: " And to
the terror and fear of said damnable persons in sign
and figure that they be accursed of God, and their
bodies committed into the hands of Satan, we have

rung these bells, erected this cross with the figure of
Christ, and as ye see this candle's light taken from the
cross and the light quenched, so be the cursed murder-
ers excluded from the light of heaven, the fellowship
of angels and all Christian people, and sent to the low
darkness of fiends and damned creatures, among whom
everlasting pains do endure."

It is very surprising to consider the vast resources
of a large chime of bells. As showing the proportionate increase accruing from the acquisition of every bell,
we find a striking illustration of the influence of the individual upon the whole. A somewhat amusing, not to
say curious calculation has been made by John Stainer,
and without taking the trouble to verify his figures, I
submit them as they stand. "Change ringing, or cam-
panology, is frequently practised when there are more
than three bells, such changes being known by the
names of Bob Majors, Bob Triples, Norwich Court
Bobs, Grandsire Bob Triples and Caters. The number
of changes a set of bells may be known by in multiply-
ing the numbers of the set. Thus three bells may ring
six changes, 123, 132, 213, 231, 321, 312; four bells
will give twenty-four changes; five bells, 120 changes;
six bells, 720 changes; seven bells, 5040 changes;
eight bells, 40,320 changes; nine bells, 362,880
changes; ten bells, 3,628,800 changes; eleven bells,
39,916,800 changes; twelve bells, 479,001,600 changes.
To ring the changes that twelve bells are capable of
would take ninety-one years at two strokes per second,
while a peal of twenty-four bells can make so many
changes that it would occupy 117,000 billions of years
to ring them all."

It would be unfair to close this sketch without presenting the reader with the size of some of the largest bells, and to that end the following list is subjoined. The great bell of St. Paul's weighs 8400 pounds. Great Tom, of Lincoln, 9894 pounds; Great Tom, of Oxford, 17000; St. Peter's, at Rome, 18,500; great bell at Erfurth, 18,114; St. Ivan's bell, Moscow, 127,836; bell of the Kremlin, 443,772. This last is the great unsuspended bell, the wonder of travellers.

One other remarkable and exclusive feature the bell possesses over every other musical instrument, and that is the lasting effect which it has had upon the human mind. Look through your library and see how many poets have written at length of any instrument but the bell. I refer to no other class of writers, because of all writers the poet is the truest interpreter of emotion. Let other men write elaborate and didactic treatises upon the organ, violin, or whatsoever other instrument, the great out-welling of the human heart breathes its " deep affection and recollection," as Father Prout has it, continuing,

> " For the bells of Shandon
> That sound so grand on
> The pleasant waters
> Of the river Lee."

To Milton, to Wordsworth and Cowper was the ringing of bells their happiness and their comfort. Tennyson could hear in their voice the ring of the Christ that is to be. Longfellow, by the ringing of the chimes of Bruges, was carried back to his own childhood's home, and woke with the happy tears upon

his cheek. But it was Poe who best understood the
moods of the bells, and he could pass from the syl-
van jingle of the sleigh bells over the frosted snow
to the voluptuous rise and fall of the golden wed-
ding bell, or starting with the startled ear of night,
portray the fierce alarum bell with all its attendant
terror and despair, full of the brazen clangor of

> " The clamorous appealing to the mercy of the fire,
> In a mad expostulation with the deaf and frantic fire,"

or passing from terror to horror, confront us with the
death tolling of the iron bell.

It is with a painful sense of its incompleteness that
I bring this paper to a close ; but it, in company with
its fellows, does not pretend to exhaust any of the subjects of which they treat. As elsewhere stated, the
object of these chapters is not to elaborate but to
condense, and by that condensation to present in a
concrete form the active principles and causes which
underlie musical history. Thus when I say of this
chapter that it is most incomplete, it may be considered
an admission for them all. But if prominent land-
marks have been brought more clearly into view, then
all that was intended has been accomplished. It will
be seen by the preceding pages that the bell, no matter
from what point of view we regard it, is a source of
endless interest. Especially to the antiquarian does
the study of bell history commend itself. There is not
nor ever was any other instrument about which clus-
tered so much of dogma, superstition, tradition and
custom. At all these things I can only hint, but if
any one better gifted for such a task should undertake

an elaborate and philosophic discussion of bell history
I feel safe in saying that the dead past will yield up
much that is now hidden, and that not only the antiquarian but the historian will find himself in possession of new and undreamed of links in the chain of
. human actions.

It has been objected, and perhaps with justice, that the manner in which the usages of bells have been treated presents no
reflection of the spiritual meaning, and that adherence to the out-
ward act and an intimation of an exclusively superstitious motive
is all that has been presented. These are matters of doctrine,
and as such become rather the province of the theologian, and
their omission implies neither ignorance of their existence nor a
wilful act having for its end their omission. Let it therefore be
borne in mind that the bell and its usages was the exclusive
object of this paper, and that while there is no attempt to ignore
any spiritual significance, the presentation of such a subject in
this place would be irrelevant and out of place.

CHAPTER X.

COLOR AND THOUGHT IN MUSIC.

THERE are many ways of saying the same thing, but there is only one best way of saying it. To know *how* best to express one's thought is a rare gift; but to know *when* to express it is a gift which confers perhaps even greater advantages upon its possessor. In ordinary life we call this tact, but in a larger sphere it is recognized as diplomacy. But while the gift of knowing *when* to speak is rarest and greatest, it is altogether dependent upon knowing *how* to speak. The right speaking at the right time is what, in a more modified sense in art, is called coloring. It is this peculiarity of coloring which distinguishes one painter from another, one author from another, one composer from another, and goes to make up the whole life of orchestration. Intellectually speaking, as every man must be regarded as a type of some class of his fellow-men (and the range is by no means limitless), and as we refer every shade of color to one of the seven prismatic colors, so by the law of derivation and material arrangement the sound of any musical instrument is its own best classification.

This word color, like so many others, is one which may be used in two different senses, either that of a cause or that of an effect. Thus, when we speak of

orchestral coloring it is not the cause to which we refer
but the effect; it is not the tone of the instrument, but
the sensation induced by the sound. Color is often
the result of association, as in the Luther chorals introduced by Meyerbeer into his opera of "Les Huguenots." In spite of all Meyerbeer's irreverent cobbling
of "Ein feste Berg," this opera derives most of its
finest dramatic effects from the introduction of this
choral, which tinges the whole play with the sense of
the impending massacre. It is strangely powerful,
this coloring, marching men on to the battle-field to
the sound of the drum and fife, up to the breast-works
where death stands waiting them. There is great
power in association, awakened by hearing a national
melody or a national instrument in a foreign land;
something grand and solemn, connected with a tune
which by consent of a great nation has been elected to
be its expression of enthusiasm and patriotism. How
many memories rise up at the sound of old melodies
that used to lead the boys to battle twenty years ago.

  A Scotchman once said to me that he would rather
hear the bagpipes than any other instrument. I
thought it bad, not to say execrable, taste. On me it
produced only the effect of sensation, but on him that
of beloved association. In the hearing of music, sensation and association are so blended as to render it
impossible to make any minute analysis. Association
remains where memory has ceased to record. We are
charmed with a melody; it frequently happens that the
charm lies in hearing again that which we no longer
remember. The memory of it has faded, but the association remains. As our lives are colored by motives

which we cannot ourselves fathom, so is all musical sound colored by some old theme which memory fails to recall. The term, descriptive music, implies a composition so highly colored, either by instrumentation, chord formations, rhythms, or perhaps all of these, as to really reflect the thought of the composer. In the days of Shakespeare, the management used to put a rock on the stage to represent the sea-shore, and a sign to convey the idea of an inn ; but the sea-shore and the tavern were but symbolized, and the audience had to depend on the text for every source of enjoyment.

The melody of the Hundredth Psalm, written long before the time of Luther, was a love ditty. The queen of Henry II. sang her favorite psalm, "Rebuke me not in thine indignation," to a fashionable jig, and Anthony, King of Navarre, sang "Stand up, O Lord, to revenge my quarrel" to the air of a dance of Poitou. Now we have on the stage the exact representation of a beach or an inn, and the skin of a horse is no longer used to symbolize that animal.

To-day we have noble chorales to sing in the house of worship, we have love-songs which convey but the one meaning they are intended to convey, and whatever may be the mood of a man, be sure he can find somewhere the song which was one day written by another man in the same frame of mind. Men want exact thinkers now-a-days in music as in philosophy. We don't want love-songs tacked on to psalm-tunes, nor sacred texts found in the company of Moody and Sankey. Just in this place I want to express my respect for all kinds of music. As in every human passion there are many degrees of intensity, in a corresponding degree we find every grade expressed in the modern song, from the lofty height of self-abnegation and devotion of Schumann and Franz down to the most slipshod twaddle of the American ballad. These represent planes of sentiment, and as such are to be respected as genuine. The true poet will ever make himself understood. The very simplest material through judicious handling produces the most beautiful and lasting result. For instance, take Rubenstein's song, the "Asra." Its elements are the simplest, yet it would be difficult in the whole range of modern Lied to find any song possessing a higher dramatic coloring. But the most astonishing economy of material is found in J. S. Bach's fifteen two-part inventions for the piano-forte. The color of an idea cannot be clearly ascertained until every change on it has been rung.

The most transcendent genius must fail inevitably, unless tutored into economy of ideas and material. He who has too many ideas is almost as poor as he who has none. The Latin proverb which bids us fear the man of one book enunciates the importance of following a thought through all its developments. When Draper wrote on the "Force of an Idea," he showed how monotheistic belief had given color to the whole Jewish thought, and through it to all modern history. This definiteness of purpose is that which gives to every work of value its merit. It is the complete whole that is required, and not a collection of graceful fragments. Strength and symmetry are the great ends to be sought in any work, great or small. To sum up, these three things are required: the right thing in the right place, to know what is most befitting the particular occasion, and how best to render it. Next to the composer of music the executive musician stands in point of merit. One of these latter may have it in his power to vitiate the taste of a whole community. This kind of people conceal the emptiness of their skulls by living on the cheap ideas of others. The true musician requires a conscience, and an active one at that. The applause elicited from the ignorant can only flatter the vulgarian. It may be objected, and with good cause, that I have used the word color as synonymous with every factor in the laboratory of music.

Indeed I am not disposed to quarrel with such a charge, but as I have considered color from a subjective, rather than an objective point, I believe that my vein is a somewhat broader one than that generally taken; and in order that there may be no obscurity in the meaning of this paper, I will restate my definition of color. It is sensation, whether that sensation be caused by rhythm, instrumentation, key, modulation, chord-formation, economy, affluence of material, tempo or shading; all alike produce sensation. The distinction is between color and ideas. The most perfect command of technique could not create an idea. With all the rhythm, all the counterpoint, all the instrumentation, all the technique in the world, you could not make a composer. And so I feel justified in saying that all which goes to make music is not music, but the material of music. Color is material, music is thought.

CHAPTER XI.

THE MODERN SONG.

WE estimate the present by contrasting it with the past. In no department of art is the spirit of the age so apparent as in that of music, and in none of its subdivisions is it stronger than in the Lied.

In fixing our attention exclusively upon the most exalted type of the German Lied, the first reflection is its characteristics : its differences and similarities —differences from, and similarities to, its predecessors ; and second, the diversities of conditions and number of individuals by which its proper rendition is imperilled. The average success of a composition is rarely in proportion to its actual merit.

Ill-balanced or untrained judgment often regards a production as with a microscope, magnifying into proportions which, by comparison, dwarf into insignificance compositions exhibiting real genius and possessing great merit. While the voice of the people must always pronounce the verdict, it is not to be trusted when pronouncing upon an innovation. The mass must be led, and the inaugurator of every upward step, especially in art, must always depend on the few for support and even existence. Such was the case of Franz, when at an advanced age he found himself confronted with poverty, and was only saved from absolute penury by the benefit concerts organized and directed by Liszt, aided by the first talent of the age.

So the evolutionized song has to struggle for its place, biding its time, but knowing that it is sure to come at last. It is to the bravery of the musicians who bring such compositions before an unsympathetic public quite as much as to their own merit that their eventual success is due, and it is to these men and women, who (for conscience' sake and devotion to the most perfect embodiment of thought) dare to encounter public prejudice and endeavor to elevate its taste, that the gratitude of every composer and executant should be ungrudgingly tendered.

In another paper I have discussed the importance and influence of art culture upon the public, and shall not enter into that here; but wherever it is encountered, this pandering to an uneducated taste and encouragement of wilful ignorance, cannot be too strongly condemned. If the admiration of a few ignorant people can outweigh a clear conscience and a sense of duty performed by the musicians, then, "Verily, they have their reward."

Our subject (that is, song) naturally subdivides itself into material and executive elements. The first involves the duties and requisites of the singer and the accompanist; the second, the consideration of the Lied proper and its text. It is then under these four heads that the Lied presents itself, and it is to their consideration, separately and collectively, that we now proceed. We have all read, talked and perhaps thought a good deal about the underlying meaning of the poet, but the question is, did we ever get at it, and if so, were we able to convey it to others? Bee-thoven somewhere said, "There are poets of tone as well as poets of words." It is of these tone poets and their meaning that I speak.

Voice.—We have all reason to thank the Lord that so few men and women are able to sing; or, whether they can or not, that so few do sing. While a good voice is the most beautiful thing in the world, it is one of the very rarest, and, moreover, requires so many accessories of mind and training that it is, after all, a questionable blessing. There are indispensable qualifications, such as accurate memory, vivid imagination, and most of all that which makes every great actor, poet, painter and author—the conception of a part. While these are the result of training, they cannot be taught. To one who has not an accurate memory no degree of excellence is possible in any department of art; but more especially does this apply in the matter of singing, for if the memory has not conquered every minor detail of pronunciation and inflection, the attention will be continually diverted from the purpose of the song to be expended upon the minutiæ which should have been mastered once for all.

The other quality upon which I have laid particular stress is the imagination. What we call feeling in singing or playing is the result of the reproduction in the mind of the performer of the subject, as it presented itself to the composer. In other words, if you would express another man's thought you must put yourself in his place. If a song has a meaning which you cannot grasp, then it were better that you should let it alone altogether. Most people sing all songs alike, and if they were actors they would play all plays alike, and to them all literature reads alike. So much is to be gotten over, and whether they be words or tones, grave or flippant, it matters little so it is done. The composer can, at the best, merely outline his meaning, and it is the privilege as well as the duty of the singer to seek for it until he has the original conception. A correct conception indicates not only analytical study, but intuition.

As has been said, these intuitive endowments must be supplemented by every physical means, the chief of which is deep, systematic and noiseless breathing. To sing well, one must be natural, but the very effort to be natural creates a constraint. "Be virtuous and you will be happy"; be natural and you will sing with ease; but it is frequently as difficult to be natural as it is to be virtuous, and while both maxims embody sound advice, they make it not one whit easier to be natural or virtuous. "A hint to the wise is sufficient." You must be on the lookout for such hints. First, judge the words by the music and then the music by the words. In this way you may the better get at the real thought of the composer. If you have a song to sing do not you sing it; try and let the composer speak through you. Be content that you are found worthy to be his mouth-piece. Do not let a spirit of egotistical impertinence lead you into adding embellishments or making omissions. Always be sure of this, if the composer knew no more of music than you he was very ignorant. If so, then he can teach you nothing; and if not, then any alteration of yours can only mar the composition. Do not bellow. All the

world is full of lunatics who think to be better liked
for their loud noise. Mezzo forte is the rule, and
pianissimo and forte impart the life-giving variety so
indispensable to every composition, great and small.

"That art of singing that abides with the *bel canto*
and is unable to sing Bach, Beethoven and Schumann
has not attained to the height of their period. It
becomes its task to adapt itself to these new circumstances, to renounce the comfortable solfeggios, and
acquire the poetic expression that they accept." The
greatest difficulty attending voice-culture is the impossibility of conveying any immediate knowledge of (if
I may be allowed the expression) throat-technique.
At the piano the teacher can place the fingers in position, but with the voice the master can only give the
quality of tone to be imitated, and so far from being
able to manipulate the muscles of the throat with his
own fingers, cannot make himself understood by the
pupil when he speaks of them. The pupil in his endeavor to imitate can only grope after the meaning,
and when he has found it will realize that it is quite as
much the result of his own search as of the example
and instruction of the teacher. It will always be so
in singing; you will never get that which you do not
yourself find. Instruction is indispensable, but the
only road to success in song is that of the earnest
seeker.

One of the most serious blemishes to which singers
of English are liable is mispronunciation. If words
are to be linked with music, they should be an object
of quite as much care as the music. It is difficult to
illustrate on paper this most common of these errors.

It is safe to say that nine-tenths of the people who pronounce correctly in conversation would never do so in singing. The reason is this : words are short tones ; the predominant sound of every word is a vowel ; the lengthening of a word is to make it become a perceptible tone. The general conversational tone is so short as to make it impossible to detect much that is impure in the pronunciation of vowels ; but the moment that we begin to lengthen them we become aware that the sounds are not pure, or that they become impure. This is particularly noticeable with the vowel i. Let any one sustain such words as light, bright, and the i will soon become an e ; or such words as clear, fire, the sound of e and i is soon lost in the vowel sound at the end of the word, and instead of e and i we have the sound er. Correct vowel singing is in fact the rarest exception ; and if any one questions this statement, let him test it by the examples given, and he will in every case find himself slipping off the pure vowel sound. Whole books of such examples could be written, but common sense and a correct ear can pick them out wherever they appear.

I shall have occasion elsewhere to speak of dead songs, but here I wish to speak of dead voices. When a voice becomes harsh or false through age or bad habits, then it cannot be considered a living voice. Do not wait for other people to tell you, but put it away (with tears, perhaps) as a mother who realizes that her baby is dead. If it was the most beautiful thing you had, then let its memory remain beautiful with all who knew it. There is no more pathetic spectacle than that of a singer who does not know that he

8

has lost his voice. I was once at a large theatre; the
singer had been great, but when he came on the stage
that night his voice broke, and for the first time he
realized that it was not what it had been. It was all
in vain that the people called him back. He only
said : " *Ce n'est plus moi, ce n'est plus moi.*"

The Accompanist.—The difficulty attending the rendition of the modern song does not lie in the voice
alone; quite as important, and much more difficult, is
the part of accompanist, and this presents a third
obstacle, for besides the difficulty of finding two persons who can attain to the inner meaning, it does not
always happen that a correct conception will be the
same, for the rendition of a song widely differing in
important details may yet leave the same impression.
If sympathy between a singer and the audience is indispensable to success, it is easy to realize the paramount importance of perfect accord between singer
and player. What the orchestra is to the chorus,
the piano is to the singer. It is this sympathy between musicians, not in the daily affairs of life, but in
the one point which characterizes them as musicians,
which raises music into a transcendental sphere where
soul lies bare to soul, and for a time individuality becomes merged into unity. When this end has been
reached, the true purpose of art is fulfilled, and all
personality is lost sight of in the nirvana of absorption.

But to return to the accompanist. To accompany
well requires not only talent but long experience. A
good accompanist is quite as rare as a good singer.
The art of accompanying is second to no branch of
music. To be a competent accompanist not only ne-

cessitates executive ability, but a knowledge of theory. It is difficult to think of intelligent playing which does not understand the laws under which it acts. Another reason why the knowledge of the theory of music is indispensable to the accompanist proceeds from the fact that he must be prepared to cover any errors committed by the singer, and to supply any omissions, without violating the rules of harmony. He must be continually on his guard against surprise from the freak, carelessness, or incapacity of the singer. He must be ready to lead or follow, as the occasion demands, and must furnish a full support for the voice, and yet never become too prominent, but always bear in mind that he only furnishes the frame and background for the picture.

Accompanying is a thankless task, for while the success of the singer is to a large extent dependent on his support, the singer always receives the credit. The duties of the accompanist are so many, and his qualifications so varied, as to make any more minute consideration of them impracticable in this space. In brief, it is his business to make manifest the powerful undercurrent of feeling which is the most marked and distinctive feature of the modern song. One suggestion more presents itself. The accompanist should always remember that no matter how insignificant or unobtrusive his part, the adherence to its letter and spirit is quite as much incumbent upon him as upon the singer.

The Lied.—It is only in our own century that the song has been elevated to its present high position. Haydn, Handel, Mozart, Gluck and their contemporaries wrote a vast number of songs, but they had

neither the breadth nor intensity characterizing the
modern Lied. In consequence, the modern German
song demands more concentration and forgetfulness
of self than it has ever claimed before. If rightly followed, the study of song is a highly intellectual pursuit. As it treats of nothing but the loftiest emotions
it demands close mental analysis and accurate interpretation.

Respectfully, yet with badly disguised indifference,
we lay aside the Lieder, which so delighted the past
generation, for the deeper glow and greater complexity
of its modern successor. "It would demand the
nature of a grave-digger to give attention to the decadence of the numerous art productions that for half a
century or more proved the delight and pride of a nation. It were unmanly, on the other hand, to close
one's eyes to the fact that even art must have its cemetery, and possesses elements that, like all earthly
things, are liable to decay, and that it were but a false
reverence ever to exhibit anew the faded robes of state
of a past age as the most precious adornment of the
present."—(From the *Tone World.*)

In an immense amount of operatic display mechanical dexterity is the only requisite to success; but in
the sensitive and highly organized modern song, the
spiritual so far predominates over the material that its
rendition is more the result of psychical than of physical accuracy. The inner meaning is too sacred to lie
on the surface to be toyed with by the mob, but like
the precious gem it represents, lies hidden, awaiting a
discoverer. The songs of Robert Schumann, Robert
Franz, Franz Schubert and their school, exhibit the

most wonderful condensation of thought ever embodied in so limited a space. "The Lied always represents a power in directing the emotions, for its province lies in seeking out intimate relations between the voice and the instrument."

Text.—"If we are to have words to music, let us subordinate the thought to the emotion. The best words to music are those which contain the fewest number of thoughts and the greatest number of emotions. Such are the shorter poems of Gœthe, of Heine, of Byron; and, as a consequence, it is notorious that Beethoven, Schubert, Mendelssohn and Schumann between them have, with pardonable avidity, set to music almost all those precious lyrics. The character of the text pretty surely indicates the quality of the music. In the union of song and poetry, insipid verses beget insipid music, just as men and women enter the marriage state by reason of their similarity of disposition. It is on the excellence of every part that the whole depends. The musician cannot write music to words which do not touch a sympathetic chord in his own nature. It is by the law of sympathy that the doctrine of natural affinity is demonstrated; and the indifference of American ballad writers as to the quality of the verses they set is the clearest indication of a low standard of musical taste and training.

"It cannot be too deeply deplored that the effect of many of our most beautiful German songs is marred, if not destroyed, by a defective translation. It may be too literal or not literal enough, or it may be, and frequently is, nothing more than doggerel. This is not always due to the incapacity of the translator, for if the idioms of our language make it difficult to translate its prose with exactness, how much more does this apply in the case of beautiful poetry? The essence is most frequently just that quality which alone cannot be translated; and while there is much to censure in the translated texts, it must always be remembered that the work is one presenting peculiar difficulties. This may serve to explain the incongruity between the text and many of the most perfect compositions.

The analogy between music and poetry as showing degrees of excellence becomes manifest when we compare such men as Schubert, Schumann and Franz, with Küchen, Gumbert and Sullivan, or such poets as Tennyson and Swinburne as compared to Rosetti and Oscar Wilde. He who selects his text at random will write random music.

In concluding so interesting a study as the modern German Lied, I beg to state that it has been written in no spirit of pedantry, but only with the wish to show its aim and relative position. If this has been accomplished it then becomes an important matter of justice to acknowledge the indebtedness of every musician, great or small, to the great outwelling of song from the heart of the people to the folk-lieder. If we are charmed by the spontaneity of Franz, bewildered by the complexity of Schumann, or thrilled by the dramatic power of Schubert; if amid the labyrinth of interlacing harmonies, we are mastered by this fervid glow and feel in them the expression of thought for which language has no equivalent and the heart no interpreter; if, coming out of these unutterable profundities we pause and ask whence come they, what is their source, and listening for answer we hear these words spoken by the seer, by Schumann himself: "Apply yourself most attentively to all popular songs. They are a mine of most charming melodies and afford an insight into the character of nations."

NOTE.—The words "popular melodies," with Schumann did not mean the song of to-day or yesterday, dying out almost in the hour of its birth, but the abiding folk-lieder of which America possesses so few, and most of them, as in the case of "Yankee Doodle" and the tune "America," imported.

"Not from the grand old masters,
    Not from the bards sublime,
Whose distant footsteps echo
    Through the corridors of time.

For like strains of martial music,
    Their mighty thoughts suggest
Life's endless toil and endeavor
    And to-night I long for rest.

Read from some humbler poet
    Whose songs gushed from his heart,
As showers from the clouds of summer,
    Or tears from the eyelids start;

Such songs have power to quiet
    The restless pulse of care,
And come like the benediction
    That follows after prayer."

"First the blade, then the ear, then the full corn in the ear." The order of every growth is from the simple to the complex; from the germ life to the fully organized existence. If ever it seems to proceed by leaps it is because the attention of the observer was

not keen enough to follow the imperceptible grada-
tions through which it expanded.   The history of music
furnishes just such an example, and the modern German song, with all its gorgeous wealth of tropical
foliage, flower and fruit, can show a lineal and honor-
able descent from melodies of the people which, in
their untutored simplicity, bring with them the resinous
odors of the pine forest, the scent of decaying leaves,
the rustle of wings among the branches, and the far-off
croon of the deep-thicketed brook.   Nature can accomplish much, but art can do more ; but nature and
art together have joined hands in the making of the
modern song, and in its limitless range of thought,
depth of sentiment, power and exactness of expression
it is at once a model of symmetry and strength.

CHAPTER XII.

"You have no idea, by the way, how much dirty work there is, to do anything at all, in music." "I suppose you mean to get at anything? But it cannot be worse than what people go through to get to heaven."—Charles Auchester. Mr. Haweis, in his little book entitled, "My Musical Memories," gives utterance to a sentiment, which, notwithstanding the fact that it is so generally entertained by most music-teachers and their pupils, I have never found in print elsewhere. "All personal relations (and teaching relations are intensely personal) have to do with subtle conditions—unexplored, but inexorable, and instantly perceived." For some reasons the position of teachers of music is, as far as it goes, a trust which involves no slight responsibility. Although rather incongruous, the most pertinent analogy which offers itself is that of the dentist. In both cases, you place yourself, or your family, in the hands of a person who, if he be not both honest and competent, will receive your money without giving the equivalent. In a common education most parents are able to form a pretty fair estimate of the amount and quality of the work their children are doing, and in a manner, every one is able to form a correct estimate of the kind of labor to which he himself has been accustomed. But set the dentist to judge of the music-teacher by his standard of dentistry, or the music-teacher to judge the dentist's work by his standard of teaching, and you will attain just about as correct an estimate of their respective merits as is usually reached by the majority of parents until some period when the work that has been done will adjudicate upon itself. Not that I would imply that parents recognize this fact; quite the contrary. The greater number not only consider themselves critics of music, but authorities on this subject, and are kind enough to advise the teacher as to his mode of instruction. This is not the result of egotism, but of ignorance. The Rev. Dr. Savage said, "It is not at all necessary that a man should ever have preached in order to be abundantly qualified to tell a minister what he ought to be and to do, to satisfy a thousand contradictory tastes and opinions. His point might be further illustrated by noticing the wisdom of unmarried people in the matter of training children. Having received a good deal of advice on this subject from unprejudiced old bachelors and old maids, I have learned thoroughly to appreciate its worth." It is very common to hear persons say: "I can detect the slightest error in music," while, in fact, the grossest violation of every musical principle would be entirely unobserved by them. It is a prevalent impression that every'one who can play music, can teach it. There can be no greater error. The science of music may be divided and classified under three heads—composition, execution and teaching. All these, as in the case of Liszt, may be combined in one individual, but such a union is by no means common. When we come to consider the amount of study involved in the grasp of any of these three divisions, the marvel is that one brain should ever be found to grasp all in one lifetime. Let us see what is required to constitute a good teacher, and by this I mean only for the piano-forte.

Harmony.—Above all he must be a student of the science of harmony, if not of the loftier branches of counterpoint and fugue. It inspires in a pupil additional respect, and while enabling the teacher to give theoretical instruction, at the same time renders him capable of detecting any errors in a composition, and explaining satisfactorily the laws and rules which make music, not as it was three centuries ago, a collection of hypotheses, but a demonstrated art, founded on fundamental laws of 'acoustics. Without some knowledge of the theory of music it is impossible for the teacher to make a correct application of the loud pedals, and this, for piano-playing, is a matter of the utmost importance. A knowledge of harmony also enables its possessor to select with judgment, and to discriminate the good from the bad, and to state wherein one composition is superior to another, and to choose, not at random or from caprice, but with a due regard to the requirements of the pupil, and always with the view of moulding and maturing his taste. Upon this fact too much stress cannot be laid, and the only means of acquiring such judgment is to be found in the knowledge of the underlying principles of music itself.

Form.—There are many other things which a

teacher ought to know. He should, at least, be sufficiently familiar with musical forms to be able to show
his pupils why a sonata is a sonata by reason of its
formation, and why a fugue is a fugue by reason of
its construction. The pupil should be taught that
these are not names arbitrarily applied to pieces, but
that they really indicate a peculiar form pertaining to
each composition thus designated. It should be understood that the symphony is but an enlarged form
of the sonata, just as the sonata is an enlarged form of
the sonatina, or the fugue of the fugetta. The subject
of musical form alone is a large one, and to be clearly
comprehended requires no little thought. These two
requisites in the music-teacher are of course only ap-
plicable to advanced pupils, but I have laid particular
stress on them, as their importance, if not their existence, is unknown to many.

Accent.—Without punctuation, written or oral language loses half its meaning. What punctuation is to
language, accent or phrasing, as it is more commonly
called, is to music. As there is no sentence without
punctuation, so there is no music without accent.
As there are many kinds of time in music, so are there
many kinds of accent. These are always divided into
two—the primary and the secondary. A correct accent cannot be too early impressed upon the pupil, as
it is the very soul of rhythm itself. There is nothing
which so clearly illustrates this as poetry. Read the
most beautiful poem without accent, and the effect of
the rhythm is altogether lost. To make understood
a correct system of phrasing, should be part of the
earliest work of every teacher.

Fingering.—I prefer foreign fingering, not that it is in itself of any particular value, but for the reason that, as all classic music is written with it, and as a vast amount of music is not written with American fingering, I think it best to use that which is most universal. This department should be studied with the greatest care, for without a correct technique no composition of any difficulty can be rendered.

Time.—All these things are so essential that the great difficulty is to say which is most important; but the inculcation of an inexorably strict time must stand among the first of the essentials. And just here I want to score a point. There are few teachers who dwell enough on the distinction between time and tempo. Time indicates the number of beats in a bar; tempo, the degree of rapidity with which it shall be played. Time may be two-quarter, four-quarter, three-eighth, six-eighth, nine-eighth, twelve-eighth and a score more; while tempo is classified and divided under five great heads—adagio, largo, andante, allegro and presto. If strict time cannot be obtained otherwise, it can be arrived at by the use of the metronome. If a correct tempo is required, most compositions of any value are metronomized, and by the use of that instrument the exact tempo of the composer can be reached.

Touch.—A good teacher is known by the touch of his pupils. A correct touch can only be acquired by long practice, and a correct position of the whole arm and hand. The touch should be both strong and elastic, so that the softest passage could be executed as smoothly as the very loudest. There are other requisites to the make-up of a good teacher, but so much has been said about those which were more important that, for fear of becoming prolix, the catalogue will end here.   But it must be remembered that we cannot catalogue the more subtle endowments which constitute the chain between teacher and taught, and stimulate to reciprocal ambition the pupil for the teacher, and the teacher for the pupil.   Now, while I claim that all these things are needful to an honest and competent teacher of the piano, I must also admit that there is no available test by which many parents could prove them to their satisfaction.   What litmus paper is to acids a diploma would be to the music-teacher.   Indeed, if both teacher and pupil could be submitted to a thorough chemical analysis, the result would in all cases, if not gratifying, be productive of good by preventing disappointment and failure.   Let us imagine such a quantitative analysis.   Pupils subjected to a chemical test of character.   Result : Dislike of study, 125 ; love of cat-worrying, 75 ; dislike of restraint, 200 ; love of riding horse-back, 198 ; dislike of music-teacher, 500 ; love of circus, 500 ; total 1598.   Quantitative analysis of teacher : Dislike to work, 600 ; dislike to pupils, 25 ; bad temper, 217 ; indifference, 411 ; total, 1253. This is what might be mildly termed incompatibility of temperament.   Supposing the analysis to be correct in the case of either party the result must be fatal to both ; for in either case the pupil will not improve, and the teacher must lose caste from having a pupil who reflects no credit upon him.   For all parties concerned, therefore, it is best that the character of the pupil, as well as that of the teacher, be studied before letting him begin.   There is still a third and most important agent to be considered in this connection. This is the parent. What the teacher does in his hour it remains for the parent to supplement during his absence. Unless this is done, it were as well never to let children begin. Music presents peculiar difficulties to the child, in that it differs from every other study by offering no daily competition with fellow-students in the presence of the whole class. It is a laborious and solitary line of study, and to this I believe that the failure of thousands must be largely attributed. The child who knows that if he misses his lesson he will receive a public reprimand, will in most instances study without being forced; but in the study of music, if the home supervision be not systematic, the music had best be abandoned as soon as possible. More failures arise from indifference of parents than from the incompetence of the teacher. This difference between teaching singly and in a body may explain another problem to which such frequent allusion is made. It is common to hear, "It costs as much for me to give my children music-lessons as to pay all the rest of their schooling put together." Very true; but do not forget that the time expended in teaching one music-pupil would have been sufficient to have taught two classes of forty each, in some other study. The training of a child in music is like unto marriage—"An estate not to be lightly entered into." It is commenced in uncertainty; it must involve years of diligent study and great expense.

Do not let it be supposed that I have overestimated the importance of a competent instructor; for under an inferior one, children contract habits which it sometimes requires years to eradicate. In this connection the Stuttgart piano-school says: " The foundation can hardly be too thoroughly laid. If the elementary instruction lacks thoroughness in a technical, musical, and especially rhythmical point of view, the result will be that afterward difficulties will be met at almost every step, and more time will be lost by stopping over details than would have been needed at first for a more thorough course of preparation." Another error into which most parents fall, is that of supposing that any piano is good enough for a beginner. A child can contract bad habits of hearing more quickly than it can those of fingering. It does not follow that the instrument used must be a new one, but it should be kept in good condition both as regards tune and action. If the piano is not in tune the child's ear will be vitiated ; and if it has not a good action, it will altogether prevent a correct touch. It is poor economy, that which is penny wise and pound foolish. Better spend no money at all than to throw it away on incompetent teachers and worthless pianos. If your child is a good one, it should be looked after twice a week ; if your piano is a good one, it deserves to be looked after once every three months, at least. In the study of music there can be no *little* mistakes. Any trivial omission in the beginning grows with the widening of the musical perception until it assumes proportions which infallibly mar, if not destroy, the beauty of every performance. The teacher must not only have good habits of rendition himself, but he must be on his guard against the ever new and vicious habits which crop out in almost every individual pupil. Many, I know, will think this whole subject has received undue consideration, but I beg to submit that, as ninety-five out of every hundred children grow up to be musical failures, there must be an ascertainable cause, and whether that cause lies with the parent, the teacher, or the child, cannot be discovered. Without co-operation of all three, failure is almost sure. Don't expect children with talent to learn without competent instruction and constant home supervision, and don't expect children without talent to learn under any circumstances.

Since writing the above, I have been advised by one far more competent to judge in such matters than myself, and it is in compliance with his advice, that I add this P. S.:

First, I refer to the development of a musical taste by the judicious selection of music by the teacher. This has been touched upon, but not with emphasis ; nor does space permit giving it the prominence which it deserves. To be able so to select is to have knowledge—of the greater part—of the field of piano music, and to be able to adapt one's self to the peculiar wants of each individual pupil. Without this knowledge and capacity, music in the hands of a teacher will rather deprave than elevate ; must injure rather than benefit.

Another point is this : If you believe your teacher competent, do not expect his lesson to bear early fruit. This green, half-ripened result is just as apt to produce mental cholera infantum as any other green fruit will cause the more common malady. There are, of course, children of exceptional talent whose progress is phenomenal ; but with the average, commencing between

9

the years of eight and twelve, it is safe to say that they will not be able to take what is commonly denominated a piece—that is, to read it—for two years, or at least eighteen months.   No one can call himself a musician who cannot read music with the same ease that he reads books.   If it takes years to acquire the ability to read books, why should it be thought strange that it should take as long, if not longer, to acquire the reading of music, which is much more complicated.   No child should be allowed to memorize a composition until it can read it at sight.   The learning of good music is like the learning of good grammar, and we acquire more of both by hearing them than in any other way.   If you have money to give in charity, remember that there are more worthy objects than you can ever minister to.   A music-teacher, as a music-teacher, is never an object of charity.   Music had best be learned altogether or not at all.   Better to have no teacher than an incompetent one.

CHAPTER XIII.

FOLK LORE.

Vox populi, vox Dei. Whether that be or not, it is well worth listening to. These stories of the people are of priceless value, growing with generations and passing from land to land, leaving their trace on the manners and customs of every nationality. In considering these traditional bequests it behooves us to remember that the subject lies behind us. The old press of John of Gutenberg was the first alarm that sounded the death-knell of tradition. Yes, the tradition song and story are being congealed into print, and this oral education may be said to have passed away. All the stories of ghosts and goblins, saints and devils, that our forefathers told, were as real to them as steam and electricity are to us now. And while we know that much they said was erroneous, we also know that it was told for truth, and their honesty has left an element of reality, lacking in the modern lore. There is pure gold in this Folk Lore, if we would only search long enough to find it. There is also a great deal of rubbish. It is to the in-lying truth what the casket is to the jewel or the husk to the nut. There are elements in this people's life of the past which on the modern stage can never be reproduced. Chief of

131

these is credulity.   Next, simplicity, and a lack of any circumlocution.   As I have said before, these were truths to them, and the unvarnished sincerity of the style was the best guarantee of the honesty of their narrators.   Beware of the man whose thought is so great that it takes him an hour to give it full expression. Ten chances to one he is piling up verbiage and stringing together platitudes, which make up the rubbish of two thirds of the sermons and lectures delivered.   It is the gift of truth to be in itself sufficient adornment. Quantity never compensates for quality.   It is in this confidence of the narrator, and the child-like directness with which he approaches his subject, wherein lies his success.   His thought, complete and vivid, is transferred to your mind and heart.   Ours are days of commentaries and text-books.   The scepticism which encounters us at every turn is a barrier to any grave assertion which does not bring with it all the credentials requisite for defence, argument and proof.   If an assertion is made, look well to your armor, for the enemy is at your gate.   Sentimentally we may deplore the disappearance of so much honest faith in such dishonest fable.   Regarded as repositories of knowledge, either direct or implied, their value is great.   We stand on the threshold of opening cycles, and no man can say what the sequence will be.   In the rush of heterogeneity the simpler elements disappear before the more complex, and the problem of the future is, How much can we combine and yet comprehend?   The road whereon we travel is one of which none may predict the end; and it is only the rough hewing, the hopeful groping in the dark, the eager reaching forward to to-morrow, and the final lying down to give room and place to another, that leads us on, on.

If the question be asked, What is folk lore? the difficulty of a direct answer is obvious, for, what is it not? If we say it is tradition, we have only half stated the case, for much of our own history is drawn from these sources. If by a paradox we attempt to cover the ground by saying pre-historic history, all the horizon becomes clouded with a chaos of gods and demigods, men and titans, and again we feel that our answer is but half complete. To apprehend the true dignity of folk lore we must realize that it is contemporary with, and antecedent to, *all* history. Not a phenomenal outburst of popular superstition of to-day or yesterday, but a continuous and unbroken chain of invention and belief, always finding a soil adapted to its perpetuation. At our end of history the scribe stands with dripping pen, ready to record the latest event. At the other end, where authentic history begins, each nation brings with it the story of an origin more miraculous than the other. Our historian at this end does not always speak truth, nor does the spokesman at the other end always speak false. The popularity of every historian is largely dependent upon the concessions which he makes to popular prejudice and popular belief. The grains of truth contained in the early narratives are sufficient alone to preserve them from oblivion.

So long as picture-writing was the only mode of recording thought, both the record and its vocabulary must have been limited; but with the birth of the alphabet, sounds, not symbols, came to be represented, and thought became literature, diffusing knowledge and formulating beliefs. The alphabet did not originate Folk Lore, but did serve to preserve many of its original outlines and more prominent features. Reaching beyond the confines of literature, folk lore discussed (satisfactorily to its generation at least) religion, geography and astronomy. These last were, however, merely the outcome of the first, for the religion which created the gods demanded a geography and an astronomy which should locate their place of habitation. " Comparative theology, which depends on the law of continuous variations of human thought, and is indeed one of its expressions, universally proves that the moment man adopts the idea of an existence of invisible beings, he recognizes the necessity of places for their residence; all nations assigning them habitations beyond the boundaries of the earth. I have not space to tell of the wonders which served to decorate the geography of those times. On the north (that is of Greece) there was the delicious country of the Hyperboreans, beyond the reach of winter; in the west the garden of the Hesperides, in which were the apples of gold; in the east the groves and dancing-ground of the sun; in the south, the country of the blameless Ethiopians, whither the gods were wont to resort. There was no river, no grotto that had not its genius; no island, no promontory without its legend."

Without any intention of discussing ancient mythology as such, it nevertheless becomes necessary to touch upon it as *one*, if not the chief and most productive source of what we denominate Folk Lore. No conception has undergone so great a change as that which the human race has entertained of God. In the Greek and Roman conception of deity, dignity does not form a leading, or even an essential component. But as Christianity grew more and more, the tricks and buffooneries of Olympus were transferred by the people to Satan and to his imps : and in the mediæval passion-plays his character is not so widely separated from the more frolicsome vagaries of the thunderer as would at first be imagined. The whole of the early Greek mythology is saturated with anthropomorphism. There is but one marked difference between gods and men ; the *one* were immortal, the *other*, mortal. The gods paid the penalty for any offences which they committed, but they could not die. They were swayed by human passions, and were made up of all human caprice and human frailty. One great difference there was between nearly all ancient and modern beliefs ; that was, the lack of any being corresponding to the devil, whose whole life was altogether given over to wickedness. There were not lacking evil and depraved spirits, but their power was not commensurate with their wickedness.

It is in Greece that the birth and growth of myth is most clearly to be traced, and it is to Greece that we look as the type of such growths in other lands. Long prior to Grecian mythology, China, Egypt and India had doubtless passed through similar stages, and this process has been repeated with greater or less variations wherever polytheism has prevailed. In every age of the world's history, and at every period of human life, a love of the marvellous has been a predominating

feature. Man is of such a nature that his curiosity
must be gratified in one way or another; and it matters
little whether that gratification be the result of demonstrated laws, or the rank fruit of the most unbridled
imagination. "What great ones do, the less will
prattle of." So every nation prattled of his maker or
makers, of whose nature they could by no possibility
have knowledge. If it was natural for men to create
a pantheon, it was also natural that its inmates should
resemble its creators. Belief in that pantheon has
never been extinguished, only its location has been
altered. All that vast system of demonology which
grew with the growth of Christianity, found in the old
Pagan polytheism material enough to stock Christendom with a full supply of devils for two thousand
years.

Old Rome languished and died of her loathsome
vices, and her power was but a shadow of the past.
Over Europe there settled a pall of ignorance and superstition, and through the darkness of that night of
the Middle Ages all things were shadowy, and every
imagination was warped by the uncertainty of its surroundings. The great highways by which alone Rome
could preserve her military supremacy, fell into decay,
and commerce and travel became the exception instead
of the rule. In the mental stagnation which followed,
it cannot be a matter of wonder that the imagination
should people its surroundings with existence both
grotesque and horrible. Belief in witches and witchcraft was as honest, and as generally entertained, as
the belief in Christianity itself. Another strong feature of popular credulity was their belief in apparitions

of the dead. These two beliefs alone were sufficiently gloomy to terrorize every community in which they were held; but here the category did not stop, and men trembled and drew close about the fire at night as they heard the Wild Huntsman rush by at the head of his terrible pack of dogs, and amid the howling fury of the winter blast. Every man believed in a personal devil, and his agency was recognized in every calamitous event. Satan was the chief of the great host of demons before alluded to, always ready to do his bidding, and, like their master, always seeking whom they might devour. But the Church, which was the first to recognize the omnipresence of the Old Harry, was not to be outdone by him, and from every monastery and convent, from the deserts of Arabia, and from all the lonely places of the earth, there poured forth the vast concourse of saints, of whose bones it might be said that, like wine, they improved with age. And so the war went on between the principle of good and evil; the imps of darkness undoing the work of the saints as soon as their respected backs were turned. Down in the mines, the leathern-eared dwarfs were busy in the preparation of explosives which ever and anon crashed down on the mortals who invaded their domain, leaving nothing but their charred corpses to tell the tale. On the coast of Gaul there were midnight knockings at the doors of the fishermen's huts, and they, rising, came forth to find their boats freighted, deep in the water, with the souls of the dead, and entering in, steered them across the channel where the unknown world was located. In some parts of Europe it was the custom to fasten the dead into their graves

by driving skewers through their bodies, and thus prevent their re-appearance.   But the full measure of
degradation was not reached until when Adrian VI.
published his famous bull against witchcraft and
sorcery.   Lecky says in the ninth century a total eclipse
of the sun struck terror through Europe, and is said to
have been one of the causes of the death of a French
king.   In the tenth century a similar phenomenon put
to flight an entire army.   More than once the appari-
tion of a comet filled Europe with an almost madden-
ing terror, and whenever a noted person was struck
down by sudden illness, the death was attributed to
sorcery.   Thus, toward the end of the sixth century
a son of Fredegonda died after a short illness, and
numbers of women were put to the most prolonged and
excruciating torment, and at last burned, or broken on
the wheel, for having caused, by incantation, the death
of the prince.   In Germany, the " Codex de mathe-
maticus et maleficus " long continued in force, as did
the old Salic law on the same subject, in France.
Charlemagne   enacted   new and   very stringent laws
condemning sorcerers to death, and great numbers
seem to have perished in his reign.   Hail and thunder-
storms were almost universally attributed to their de-
vices, though one great ecclesiastic of the ninth century,
Agobard, archbishop of Lyons, had the rare merit of
opposing the popular belief.   " Sprenger computes that
during the Christian epoch no less than nine millions
of persons, mostly women of the poorer classes, were
burned for witchcraft."

The air was dense with superstition to which the
monks added continually by their legends of the saints,

and the miracles produced through their interposition. These were, at least, a contrast to the demonology of the age, and presented a brighter picture to terrorized humanity. There was, as there has been from time immemorial, the belief in fairies ; and to these nursery tales men listened with a credulity scarcely surpassed by the four-year-old of to-day. "Once upon a time." "And they lived happily ever after." Those two clauses, the one at the beginning, the other at the end of our nursery joys, doubtless imparted greater pleasure a thousand years ago than they do to-day. Fortune-telling was a very serious matter, more often to the teller than to the told, for any dealing in the black art was a road which generally found its terminus at the stake. There·was a pot of gold at the end of the rainbow, and there was any amount of buried treasure, if only one could find it. It would be pleasing to linger over these playful imaginings, but where so large a subject is to be considered, it becomes a matter of necessity to economize space.

An intrinsically valuable department of the Folk Lore, because of its epigrammatic embodiment of truth, are all those pithy sentences and couplets which, from their general acceptation and constant use by the common people through all the world, have come to be known as proverbs. I say intrinsic, because while legend and myth are of incalculable value to the philologist, furnishing clews and links which in the family of languages must otherwise be lacking, they do not in themselves embody any self-evident truth as do the proverbs, and can, at best, rank no higher than clever fables. The proverb appeals to our common sense, but

the narrative to the imagination.   In Folk Lore we
might almost say that the one is remembered by reason
of its truth, and the other by reason of its falsity.
Doubtless every story had its foundation, no matter
how slight, in some actual occurrence, but under the
comparatively imposing superstructure which soon
arose, the foundation was lost sight of; while the proverb, admitting of no such superstructure, remained,
and always will remain, the common-sense exponent of
every-day life.   That a saying, or narration, has become Folk Lore by becoming common property, by no
means implies a common origin.   It is to Bishop
Trench's work on proverbs that I am indebted for the
following examples.   I instance a few which speak with
such clearness as to be their own best commentary.
"He who waits for dead men's shoes may go bare-
foot."   A yet more lugubrious one says, " Every door
may be shut but death's door."   Another, back as far
as the fourth century, says, "One must not look a gift-
horse in the mouth."   Another of equal antiquity says,
"Liars should have good memories."   From the Span-
ish we have the following sanguinary proverb :—" Kill,
and thou shalt be killed, and they shall kill him who
kills thee."   A companion to this is to be found in the
Italian, which says, "Revenge of a hundred years old
hath still its sucking-teeth."   The English proverb,
" Gray hairs are death's blossoms," seems to find a
fitting sequel in that of the Turk, " Death is a black
camel which kneels at every man's gate ; " and this
may possibly be yet farther extended to that from the
Arabic, "There are no fans in hell."   A somewhat
consoling proverb comes to us from the Chinese, to

any who may wish to appropriate it:—"Towers are
measured by their shadows, and great men by their
calumniators." Say the Italians, "Silence was never
written down, and there is no worse robber than a bad
book;" and also, "He has need of a long spoon who
eats with the devil." I will give but one more, which
is from the Arabic, and combining both wisdom and
poetry:—"Every day in thy life is a leaf in thy history." In glaring contrast to all this cut-and-dried
wisdom I now present some witty frivolities which have
certainly a right to be classed as folk lore.

This is what is known as "cant" in England, liter-
ally meaning "thieves' dialect," but in this country
comprehended under the head of "slang." While the
English mind has been very prolific in this kind of
coinage, it has been sadly lacking in the wit which imparts to the slang of other lands vivacity and humor;
and it is for this reason that I omit any quotations
from the English. The French slang for prison is
"College" or "Abbays de Sots," the college or fool's
abbey. The gibbet is "Veuve," the widow. To suf-
fer capital punishment, "Epouser la Veuve," to marry
the widow. To eat, "Jouer des Dominos," to play
dominoes. And the sea is, "La grande Tasse," the
large cup. Rain, "Bouillon de Chien," dog soup.
The moon is "Moncharge" or "Cafarde," female spy.
An Englishman, "God dem." In the Gypsy cant a
priest is "Schwarzbarbar," black dyer. In the dialect
of Germania a highway robber is picturesquely called
"Ermitano de Camino," the hermit of the road. A
man hanged is spoken of as "Racimo," a bunch of
grapes. Wit and wisdom are not always characteristic

of Folk Lore. All languages abound in sayings and couplets which preserve themselves rather by their jingle than by the embodiment of truth. Many of these were born, and live, and will continue to live, for the benefit of the little people. So we may be said to have a lore corresponding in its babbling to the ears it is intended to tickle.

The following, taken from the celebrated work entitled, "Notes and Queries," will serve to illustrate :

> "On Candlemass Day if the sun shines clear,
> The shepherd would rather see his wife on the bier."

Says another :—

> " As far as the sun shines in on Candlemass Day
> So far will the snow blow in before old May."

There is an old monastic proverb on the same theme :—

> "Si sol lucescat Maria purificante
> Majus frigus erit post quam erat ante."
>
> " If the sun shines on Mary's purification
> There will be greater cold after than before."

And yet another :—

> " When Candlemass Day is come and gone,
> The snow won't lay on a hot stone."

Antiquaries may be able to find beauty in the following lines, but I confess myself incapable of so much enthusiasm :—

> "Shroving, shroving, I am come to shroving :
> A piece of bread, a piece of cheese,
> A piece of your fat bacon,

Doughnuts and pan-cakes
All of your own making.
Shroving, shroving, I am come to shroving."

A somewhat different version of Marjory Daw is
found in Cornwall, the Pixies alluded to being a species of fairy abounding thereabout :—

" See-saw, Marjory Daw
Sold her bed and lay upon straw ;
Sold her straw and lay upon hay,
Pixies came and carried her away."

But two of these amiable little people are known by
name, and they are thus alluded to :—

" Jack o' the Lantern ! Joan the Wad !
Who tickled the maid and made her mad,
Light me home, the weather's bad."

One more, and I shall have done with these exhausting productions :—

" White bird, featherless,
Flew from Paradise,
Pitched on the castle wall ;
Poor Lord Landless
Came in a fine dress,
And rode away horseless."

By reason of the curious conceit I am led to add yet
one more :—

" A row of white horses
Sat on a red hill.
Now they go, now they go,
Now they stand still."

This is the picture, for the babies, of white teeth on
red gums.

Leaving behind all these fragmentary embodiments
of thought of the people, we must again turn our attention to the vast repository of Folk Lore proper, comprised under the head of Myth and Legend. In a
sketch of this kind, the merest outlines of the subject
only may be given. The material and variety are so
abundant as to make the task of a comprehensive, and
yet condensed presentation a difficult one. Through
all the vast field of history, directly or indirectly, we
can trace the powerful influence of myth and legend.
The savage mind, not content with personifying the
powers of good and the powers of evil as individuals, sub-created an innumerable host which have held
their place through all time, and, to a large extent,
continue to do so. If our own language is so rich in
names for this unseen world, we may readily believe
that in this respect it is only the counterpart of others.
That Paganism should be Christianized was not
enough, but as has been said before, we have Christianized their myths also. The demons, dryads, har-
pies, wizards and sirens have only changed names, and
been baptized over in the popular belief, and modern-
ized, and remodelled into fairies, gnomes, goblins,
elves, pixies, and a thousand others, not to speak of
an innumerable company who possess only a local
reputation. Saturated with the spirit of modern criticism, we cannot enter into the world where our fathers lived. We can no more be magnetized by its
mysteries than we are to be frightened by its terrors.
Intelligence and incredulity have marched side by
side through the whole history of the human race;
and these stories, which still receive credence among

the vulgar to an unrealized extent, will continue to be preserved as long as ignorance predominates. The imagination which peopled earth, air and ocean with existences, some favorable, some inimical to the interests of man, is now directed to tracing the origin and development of such fantasies. The most striking illustration of the decline of the belief in Mythology and Demonology is to be found in the almost phenomenal disappearance of any belief in witchcraft. The good old custom of burning a woman because some one else's cow broke her leg, or a child was sick, or the sheep had the rot, or the butter wouldn't come, has quite passed out of existence, and the high-cockolorum and the broomstick are become a part of the past; but the myths remain, and while we cannot reverence them as oracles, we can at least pay them the respect due to antiquity, and it is with a reverent rather than a curious disposition that I approach their discussion.

I am the more encouraged in this spirit by the following passage from the little book called "The Origin of Myth." Mr. Clodd says, "In this" (that is, Folk Lore) "lies Primitive Philosophy, Theology and Science, the beginnings of all knowledge that has been and that ever will be." A belief, whether founded on a demonstrable basis, or existing merely as a hypothesis, is the cause of all action. All religion has for its foundation the belief in its founder or founders. Religion and superstition have been sadly mixed up in men's minds, and it is not strange that they should have been often mistaken, the one for the other, thus giving to superstition as great an authority for good or ill as

possessed by religion. It would be idle to discuss so
self-evident a fact, as the paramount influence of religion over the race is indisputable ; but as all religion,
to a large extent, is founded on narrative, it is to these
narratives that we must look as the power behind the
throne. Call these myths if you choose, but remember
that they are the sum of the factors that made *you*
what you are. As factors in making history they are
quite as important as the greatest historical events,
and let it never be forgotten that the faith in a false
creed has quite as much longevity and power of execution as that possessed by a true faith.

If the object of this paper was to become the thorough exponent of any one of the branches under which
Folk Lore naturally divides itself, the length of that
one subject alone would fill a volume, possibly many.
If, in what has preceded, passages have been cited to
exemplify certain forms of Folk Lore, it was either on
account of their epigrammatic or fragmentary nature.
Of the myths and legends it is only permitted to me
to speak, not to illustrate. The highest guarantee of
the value of such data is to be found in the opinion of
the men from whom I shall now quote. From the little book just cited, "The Origin of Myth," Mr. Clodd
says :—"The application of the scientific method to
the study of man has given a wider meaning to the
word 'myth' than that commonly found in the dictionary. These explain it as a fable, as designedly
fictitious, whether for amusement only, or to point a
moral. The larger meaning which it holds to-day includes much more than this; to wit, the whole area of
intellectual products which lie beyond the historic

horizon and overlap it, effacing, on nearer view, the lines of separation." In another place he says:— "One thing is certain, that language was once the scene of an immense personification," and has thereby added vitality to myth. Says Keary:—"The world is all before them where to choose. Nature, in her multitudinous works and ever changing shows, is at hand to give breath to the faculty of myth-making, and lay the foundation for all the stories which have ever been told." Mr. Gould in his " Curious Myths of the Middle Ages," thus epitomizes a number of legends, and I can do no better than to quote him at length. " John the Divine slept at Ephesus, untouched by corruption, with the ground heaving over his breast as he breathed, waiting the summons to come forth and witness against anti-Christ. The Seven Sleepers reposed in a cave, and centuries glided by like a watch in the night. The Monk of Hildesheim doubting how with God a thousand years could be as yesterday, listened to the melody of a bird in the green wood during three minutes, and found that in three minutes three hundred years had flown. Joseph of Arimathea, in the blessed city of Sarras, draws perpetual life from the Saint Grail. Merlin sleeps and sighs in an old tree, spellbound of Vivian. Charlemagne and Barbarossa wait, crowned and armed, in the heart of the mountain, till the time come for the release of the Fatherland from despotism. And on the other hand, the curse of a deathless life has passed on the Wild Huntsman because he desired to chase the red deer forever more; on the captain of the phantom ship because he vowed he would double the Cape whether God willed it or not; on the Man in the Moon because he gathered sticks during the Sabbath rest; on the dancers of Kolbeck because they desired to spend eternity in their mad gambols." These are only examples of the material of which myths are made, and must be classed, as does Mr. Gould, as rather curious than valuable.

The real value of a myth depends on its antiquity and general diffusion. To the groping of the primeval mind the deifying of nature was a step which it required no highly colored imagination to take. The next step was as inevitable as the first had been natural. The gentle rain descended, and beneath its warming, softening influence the ground parted as. by magic, and the sweet, warm moisture drew from the fertile earth the fruits and cereals without which all intellectual life must soon pass away. Out of the same sky burst the tempest, wind, hail, thunder and lightning, and all that the kindly rain had done was in a moment obliterated. The sun shone down, and under his genial rays animal and vegetable life alike rejoiced; but the sun departed to be succeeded by gloom and darkness. Was it possible that the terror inspired by such phenomenon on the one hand, and the joy by that on the other, could be the emanations of one and the same being? No, the semi-barbaric mind rejected the proposition with scorn, and thus was taken the second and inevitable step, and from worshipping nature as a whole, men turned to personifying her in accordance with her different attributes. In this connection Keary says:—" We may expect to find myths relating especially to the labors of the sun, like those of Heracles and Thor; or to the wind, like that of Hermes stealing the cattle of Apollo; or to the earth sleeping in the embrace of winter, or sorrowing for the loss of her greenery, or joyful again in her recovered life." Can we wonder that about the sun-god there gathered more and more a halo of loving tradition? Can we wonder that men shrank with terror and abhorrence from *his* foes who seemed momentarily threatening him and the whole human race with destruction, and the universe with chaos? Abhor it as we may, can we wonder that to the terrified belief of the conscience-stricken savage even human sacrifice seemed not too great a propitiatory offering to avert from the race such a calamity? Thus there came into being a priesthood and a ritual, and the masses looked to them for strength and aid when all else failed. This was a power greater than that of the monarch, and these were the beliefs by which men shaped their lives. A power within a power is a dangerous institution, and when they clashed, then came the making of history. And the priest said, as he has in later days also: "Give to me the power over man's conscience, and it is but a question of time and opportunity and I will own him, body and soul." And now, behold! the vague groping of man after the unknowable has formulated itself into the written law of millions; alike the support of despotism, and the consolation of the dying beggar.

These are generalities, but the student of history will no more question them than he will question the magnitude of their influence. There is something very impressive in thus contemplating the history of history. This standing, as it were, with the primeval page

dimly outlined before us.   What a subject for the student of paleontology.   Link after link slowly brought
to light, and gradually evolving the chain of cause and
effect, and carrying us, by a pathway hitherto undreamed of, back to the beginning of human history.
History indeed repeats itself, but the repetitions take
place in ever widening circles.   And what makes up
the substance of these ever recurring cycles?   Most
truly many things ; but I believe that these may be
summed up under two heads : the warped and fallible
judgment of man, forever warring with his lofty striving after a greater good.   Like most morals, that contained in the history of Folk Lore is one which is so
obvious as to need no pointing.   First, the egotism
which could assign a cause without a sufficient basis
for belief; second, the credulity which could accept
that cause as truth; and third, the fallibility of the
judgment which finally formulated that belief into a
dogma.   Little did he dream, who gave the impetus to
the first stone of mythology, that it should roll and
roll, never pausing till it had gathered about it material sufficient to rear the vast and imposing structure of
polytheistic belief.   Standing at a later day, we can
better estimate the energy of the forces then set in
motion and better judge of their titanic workings.
Like the volcanic fires which forever burn beneath our
feet, they have upheaved whole continents, and sub-
merged others.   Standing amid the wrecks of dead
empires, of dead civilizations and of dead religions, we
must yet admit that the spirit which brought them into
existence has not died out, but, like the volcanic fires,
still smoulders beneath our feet, and the leaven bred

of ignorance and superstition may yet burst forth in a more lurid and more awful cataclysm than the world has ever seen. The seed-time of one age makes the harvest of the next. Unconsciously the woof of myth, tradition and legend has been woven, and beneath the unity of purpose in, and detail of, its far-reaching fibres all humanity is enfolded, and the lore which points to a common origin points alike to a common history and a common destiny. To what is it that we listen? Is it the voice of a man? Of a class? Of a nation? Verily, *no;* but the fathomless, boundless chant of the myriads that have preceded us, and the myriads following in their footsteps. Vox populi, vox Dei.

CHAPTER XIV.

EMERSON once said, in substance, that the greatest literary defect was a lapse into the commonplace. In a recent address, Mr. Lowell said, in substance, we cannot overrate our debt to those things which are commonplace. Here is a discrepancy. But there may be a good many paths to the top of the same mountain, and two men may travel in opposite directions, and yet meet on the summit. When Emerson condemned the commonplace, he did not condemn the common. When Lowell commended the commonplace, I think he confused the idea of the commonplace with the common. Our ideas of the common and the commonplace, so far as their likeness and dissimilarity are concerned, are not as easy to express as to appreciate, and by this I mean that no language has ever been adequate to the task of formulating into words, those subtleties of intuition, which we call trains of thought. The common may be commonplace, and the commonplace may be common; but the qualities which distinguish each, will, in their very fusion, disclaim affinity. What, then, *is* the difference between common and commonplace? The word common is the most ill used in the English language. Common, in the general acceptation, denotes some-

152

thing unattractive, plain, as when we say a common house, or a common man or woman. By this we do not mean that the house, man, or woman are property common to the public, or even that their similarity to other houses, and other men and women, makes them a type of a class. Either of these uses would be correct; but in the manner in which it is used we seem to have a whole staircase of commons, reaching up from all kinds of meanings placed on the word, to what I consider the loftiest, noblest common.

Strictly, there is but one meaning to the word common: it is that which, under the great democracy of humanity, has become the general inherited *possession* of mankind. To be common is to be as the ocean that rolls its waves impartially under the equatorial sun, and in the mysterious unknown of the northernmost polar sea. To be common is to be as the Gulf Stream, as it coils about the world, holding it in its encircling grasp like a beneficent serpent. To be common is to be like the winter as it lays its iron hand upon nature, in the dumb foreshadowing of a greater catastrophe. Common is the mother rejoicing over her babe. Common is that mother as she stands by the grave of her babe. To be common is to be as life, as death, as love, as hate. It is to be as the sunshine giving life and gladness wherever it rests; or as the rain which falls in due season, sending the warm life through the veins of all nature; or as the plague, pestilence, famine, battle and murder, leaving in its wake a pathway charred and blasted. All these things are common, but none commonplace. All nature, in the broadest sense, is common; but *there* is nothing commonplace.

Every man, consciously or unconsciously, defines certain words in his own peculiar manner; and my definition of the commonplace is the *threadbare*. Threadbare from the constant use, and from its everlasting sameness. Some kinds of cloth are a good deal harder to rub threadbare than others, but if you rub long enough you will get the gloss off, and the shiny smoothness will make its appearance. Sometimes this cloth is mightily freshened, by being put away for a long time and then brought out, just as in literature, books are often laid aside for one or two generations, and come out looking fresher than ever. Real honest love, and real honest hate, are never threadbare, because they, like nature, are forever presenting new phases. To the individual himself, life is never commonplace, inasmuch as each day brings (it may be in a trifling degree) some new phase of living, or some novelty. Death is never commonplace, and for many reasons : men do not die alike any more than they live alike, and the last act of a man's life, that is, his dying, is remembered when many more important ones are forgotten. It is the sham death, the sham life, the artificial nature, that is commonplace. Nature is, after all, the great teacher and exemplar. Whether for our good or ill, she makes no distinction in favor of a class or creed, but her rain falls alike upon the just and the unjust : the common mother to the common humanity. Therefore when we seek the commonplace, it must not be in the writing on the primeval page of nature ; but, turning from her, we must look for it in the hearts of men.

Look at their sayings and doings ; at their vulgarities and littlenesses. We shall see wherein the common may or may not be commonplace. We shall neither be wasting time splitting hairs, nor dealing with abstract subtleties. It is the peculiar province of a man that he may go into himself, as into a house, and having shut to the door, look into the condition and character of the furniture of his mind and heart. It is not only his peculiar province, but his highest privilege and most bounden duty. Well is it for such an one if, when he looks about him, he shall find nothing in that furnishing which is not in accordance with the great commonalty of humanity without.

I have stated before that common doesn't mean the good, any more than it means the bad; but it is neither little nor puny. It stands up, strong and lusty, and speaks with a voice that can be heard above the little voices about it, and says, "I hate, I love." O strong hate and love ! Both perhaps right, both perhaps wrong; nothing can adjudicate upon them but the causes which lie behind. Viewed in this aspect, a man ceases to be a type, but is representative nature. His lawless passion, riding down every bulwark of society, and brooking no barrier, is as swift and as fierce as the maelstrom grasping its victim, and hurrying it down to satisfy its unsatiable and unnatural appetite. Lawless this, *very*, but common; common as the race, and as nature. How many men have written on Napoleon Bonaparte ! how many men have denounced him ! But with all their writing, there is something within them of which they themselves are not aware. O the frailty of humanity! and therein we are not like nature, for we would do that which we cannot.

You men who pile up volumes in condemnation of the conqueror of Europe, what is it that you lack? Ambition? No. Pride? No. Self-love? No. Arrogance? No. What, then?   O mockery! the one thing that made Napoleon what he was—ability! What is it that makes your pulses thrill when you read of the conqueror in Leipsic, in Vienna, in Moscow, in Berlin, in Brussels, now in the high Alpine heaven, now in the valleys of Italy; standing where forty centuries look down upon him, or making himself crowned head of half the world : what is it but admiration?   Conceal it from yourself if you will, it is there ; and, with the proper environment, would bear fruit of which you little dream.   Yes, it is the fellow feeling, given certain conditions, and certain results will follow which proclaims our oneness in the life which is common to all.   But you say, Napoleon was commonplace in his littlenesses.   What of that? *they* never made him great.   Every littleness that that conqueror had was commonplace, yet they were common.   Every act of heroism, every deed of patriotism, every story which tells of a deep-laid plot of revenge carries us with it.   Read again the story of William the Conqueror.   Read again the story of Harold, the defender of his country.   No matter which, our hearts go forth to them.   It is our double self proclaiming itself first on one side, and then on the other.   It is our common feeling, asserting itself on either side. Go back as

The Common and Commonplace.   157

far as you will—Cataline against Cicero, and .Cicero
against Cataline. Cæsar against Pompey, and Pompey against Cæsar. Savonarola against the Pope,
the Pope against Savonarola.   John of Barnavelt
against Maurice of Orange, and Maurice against John.
Guelph against Ghibelline, Ghibelline against Guelph.
You will find men of to-day taking sides, not on facts
but with factions. Take the case of the British occu-
pation of India. How we all sympathize with the native princes and their subjects, bound hand and foot
under the British yoke : and yet what pleasure it gives
us to see the dominion of the white man reach over
the land of India. These are paradoxes; and yet
they are common to us all, and indisputable.

What though the silence of annihilation brood forever over the halls of the Montezumas ? What though a
civilization of equal development as that of Mexico
was wrested from the hands of the Incas, and not shat-
tered, but distilled into nothingness ? What though
heaven be shaken with the outcry of the down-trod-
den millions ? What though the earth be strewn with
their corpses, and the rivers run thick with their blood.
though the sky be black by day, and blazing by night,
with the conflagration of a thousand villages ? What
of the hundreds of thousands, dying and rotting, deep
down in the mines, goaded on by the whip of the hell-
hound Spaniard to satisfy his insatiable lust for gold?
Weep over them, deplore them, put in your share of
pity with your common humanity. Say, "He was my
brother ; this was his life, his home, his land, his blood,
his ruin," and then ask your heart how much you have
kept back for the men who did all this devil's work

Ask how much admiration, how much hero-worship. O the brave Castilian! O the chivalric Spaniard! look at him. For every man, a thousand foes. March on, conqueror, by the beacon fires which thine enemies have kindled for thy destruction. How exhausting your marches! how valiantly fought your battles! how overwhelming your victories! A handful of men against a whole nation. Blood! blood! Is he not defending his life? Help for Cortez! help for Pizarro! no time to be lost. But see! O wonder! O glory! O marvel, not of the age but of all time! they overcome, they conquer. Now let your common motherhood assert herself, and, for lack of your own glory, glory in the glory of another type of your race. Ah, defeated people, we weep with you, and in our hearts we raise up monuments to your memories, for are you not human, and might not your misfortunes have been ours? But, O conqueror, we joy with *you*, for the crown of glory sits upon your banner, and we triumph in your victory.

Wonderful is this commonness, in its ability to look at both sides, even in this posthumous way. Common to be condemned, common to be glorified. Common to be in earnest, commonplace to be the threadbare object of toleration, if not of contempt. To be both common and commonplace is to be weak; to be common is to be strong; to be commonplace is to be vulgar and meaningless. Whatever lacks character,—whatever has stamped on its face insipidity,—whatever does not convey to us a meaning and a purpose—that is the true commonplace. Cortez, Pizarro, fight on! conquer! Aztec, Peruvian, defend your homes as best you may!

Your fight began with the first memory of man, and it will not end till his last memory. Nothing commonplace here, in the *court* which the Spaniard has left behind him. He may one day again form part of it, but that is no concern of ours, for we have to do but with the struggle, which is the typical struggle of all the race. Common, common, gloriously common this strength, this weakness. It is this effort to balance the accounts of the ages, by standing first on one side and then on the other; that is the common effort of the race.

The common ground on which we stand is becoming broader, and more men are thinking their own thoughts than ever did before, and there is more of an effort to reach out and help others to the highest level of common humanity. What is it to us that the land is flooded, like the sand on the sea-shore, with the froth and tinsel of journalistic platitudes. Much that is good must drop through the sieve of public opinion; but if a man is really in earnest, and withal, has something worth the hearing, he will not long lack an audience. In the world of mental forces there are only a certain number of truths to be known, and, in this respect, there is nothing new under the sun. But turning from the purely intellectual, to the influence of the immaterial over the material, we stand immediately in the presence of those mental processes, formulated, and crystallized into matter. The Pharaohs raised the pyramids, that they might thereby preserve their memory; history has set her seal of rebuke upon those proud monarchs, by obliterating that memory. The thought of preserving their memories was as small as the thought of building the pyramids was large. The man who can be remembered by nothing better than a pile of stone, were best forgotten. Yet the pile of stone stands, and we glory in it. Not as the work of part of the race, but as part of the work of the race.

I trust I may not be considered irreverent in speaking of these piles, when I say that our admiration is excited, not so much by their immensity as by the fact that our race built them. After all, if we were in search of size, whereby we might be overawed, we would not go to the pyramids at all, but go and look up the first respectable mountain, near at hand. Ah, if we had only built the mountains, then our laudations of the race, and our pride in the race, never would have known limits. Pyramids, temples, shorn of your glory, standing in your lonely grandeur in Thebes, in Memphis, Baalbec, Nineveh, Rome, Athens, your children have returned to the earth from whence they sprang, and ye stand, childless and bare, amid the memories which alone make you what you are! Power, wealth, beauty,—they have all held sway over the earth, and have each in turn left their trace, and bequeathed their influence and their exhortation to the children of *their* children. But if these things were found in nature, would we wonder over them? Do you want power? Go to nature. Do you want wealth? Go to nature. Do you want beauty? Bow down in voiceless wonder before the unspeakable glory which men may not even imitate. Heaven and earth, sun, moon, and stars, sea and mountain, tempest, volcano, and earthquake,—these are the pigments, the elements, and the ministers of her will. Nature builds as a giant;

men build as pigmies. And yet there has been a whole library written to commemorate the deeds of men, where one page has been written to tell the wonders that are in nature. This is right, this is just, for she is no part of us though we be part of her. I would rather be possessed of one of the Aztec manuscripts, destroyed by the Spaniards in the square of the city of Mexico, than to be owner of a universe of rainbows. I would rather have the library destroyed at Alexandria than to be possessor of the solid golden peacock's throne. Better to have been the discoverer and interpreter of the Rosetta stone than to have been Rothschild.

We want to know who were our common fathers and mothers. What did they do as they stood on the threshold of history? I had rather hold the key to that history, than to hold the key to the Cosmos. We cannot too earnestly search nature, that we may wrest her secrets, and thereby triumph over her. Love nature for all she is worth, but love your fellow man for your common origin, and common brotherhood. I think I have said enough of the commonplace to enable me now, and finally, to let so unpleasant a subject rest, in order to devote the remainder of our time to the consideration of the truly common in humanity.

As I have said before, in substance, to be common is to represent the striving of the race; and the main current of that striving is not downward, but upward. The strong tendency is not for evil, but for good. It would be difficult to-day to find many Roman Catholics who would justify the massacre of the Eve of St. Bartholomew; the sack of Constantinople, the capital of

11

the Greek Church ; the extirpation of the heresy in the
south of France, nor the working of the Holy Inquisi-
tion. Protestantism has less to reproach itself with,
partly because it was the product of a later age, partly
because its life has been shorter and its opportunities
fewer, and partly because the responsibility of any
overt act could not rest on a Church which had no
temporal head, but on the individuals by whom it was
committed. The Protestant is as loath to endorse
such acts as the Catholic. We, as a race, stand on a
higher ground than we did four centuries ago. If we
do not repudiate, we do not endorse the crimes of our
ancestors. This article does not treat of causes, but
of results. I am not now discussing the question,
whether it is to the Church, or to a greater freedom
of thought we owe our enfranchisement. Those are
questions which belong rather to the theologian and
logician, and have no bearing on the subject under
discussion.

The world is full of blessed memories, and of what?
Of good men, blessed because they were good. Have
you any blessed memories connected with a *bad* man?
These are the memories common to us all, that come
to us like the very voice of God. Show me the man
who has no such memories, and I will show you a bes-
tial savage. Back, back, over the broad and fertile
fields of history, where the first streaks of the rising
sun may just be seen; back where the twilight is just
beginning to appear, yes, even into the awed hush of
the primeval morning of history, these inherited memories carry our hearts. All history ought to be dear
to us, for it is indeed written in the blood of the race.

How reverentially we should approach it, this common story of our common destiny. You can hear them marching, their bugle-calls, and the roll of their drums. But we need not look so far back for ideals. We need not go to Thermopylæ for heroes, nor seek the religious philosopher in Marcus Antoninus, or Epictetus. All along the pathway where men. have trodden they have planted these memories, which have flourished like bay trees, by the rivers of water. They never died; they are all living and real. Take the great men, good in the main, because their work for the race was good in the main : Clovis, Charlemagne, Alfred, William, Charles Martel, Wellington, Washington.

Crash, roar, battle everywhere ; but, lo ! as the white heart, said to have been found among the ashes of Joan of Arc, so comes out humanity : not exactly, nor half, nor to any very great extent white, but whiter, getting whiter every day. How many common memories we have of teachers and reformers, ministers of governments, and of God. How great is our common love for the men who write our books for us. The men who do our thinking, and our talking. What a pleasure it is to be part of a race that lays claim to such men. Our common boast is, that we can go faster, and talk further, than ever before. Our great buildings are not for show, but for use. . Our railroads, reaching for thousands of miles ; our bridges, spanning great estuaries ; our leviathan ships, our prodigious commerce, our giant machinery, astronomy, chemistry, law, medicine,—these are all sources of just pride and joy to us all.

" Men my brothers, men the workers, ever reaping something
   new,
   That which they have done but earnest of the things that
   they shall do."

We are only standing in the doorway of our common
house. Co-operation was never so general, discipline
never so perfect. As the unparalleled diffusion of
knowledge and civilization is chiefly due to our increased facilities of communication, it follows that,
with these facilities ever increasing, the spread of
knowledge must be in equal ratio.   Our fathers are
dead, but they built for us. Shall we fear to be step-
ing-stones for those who come after? Community of
sentiment means community of interest. If we look
back with pride upon what the race has done, we may
well look forward with child-like wonder to what the
race·shall do. The representative man is the common man. Not by reason of his clothes, his face,
speech, or manners, but in his thoughts and deeds.
Scoff at the suggestion if you will, but altruism, the
true commonism, which loves its neighbor as itself,
and makes common cause against all men *for* all men,
is the greatest growth of the age.   In this republic of
mind, the highest boast that you can make is, that you
stand in the rank of the grand army ; that your
brother's cause is your own, even as yours is his.
The battle-field is great, and the battle will be long ;
but the men who have hearts common enough to fight
for, and to lay down their lives for common humanity
will be victorious at last, and be counted among the
commonest blessings of the human family.

The Story of the Nations.

MESSRS. G. P. PUTNAM'S SONS take pleasure in announcing that they have in course of publication a series of historical studies, intended to present in a graphic manner the stories of the different nations that have attained prominence in history.

In the story form the current of each national life will be distinctly indicated, and its picturesque and noteworthy periods and episodes will be presented for the reader in their philosophical relation to each other as well as to universal history.

It is the plan of the writers of the different volumes to enter into the real life of the peoples, and to bring them before the reader as they actually lived, labored, and struggled—as they studied and wrote, and as they amused themselves. In carrying out this plan, the myths, with which the history of all lands begins, will not be over-looked, though these will be carefully distinguished from the actual history, so far as the labors of the accepted historical authorities have resulted in definite conclusions.

The subjects of the different volumes will be planned to cover connecting and, as far as possible, consecutive epochs or periods, so that the set when completed will present in a comprehensive narrative the chief events in the great STORY OF THE NATIONS; but it will, of course, not always prove practicable to issue the several volumes in their chronological order.

The "Stories" are printed in good readable type, and in handsome 12mo form. They are adequately illustrated and furnished with maps and indexes. They are sold separately at a price of $1.50 each.

The following is a partial list of the subjects thus far determined upon :

THE STORY OF EARLY EGYPT. Prof. GEORGE RAWLINSON.
   "   "   " *CHALDEA. Z. RAGOZIN.
   "   "   " *GREECE. Prof. JAMES A. HARRISON,
                                Washington and Lee University
   "   "   " *ROME. ARTHUR GILMAN.
   "   "   " *THE JEWS. Prof. JAMES K. HOSMER,
                                Washington University of St. Louis.
   "   "   " *CARTHAGE. Prof. ALFRED J. CHURCH,
                                University College, London.
   "   "   " BYZANTIUM.
   "   "   " THE GOTHS. HENRY BRADLEY.
   "   "   " *THE NORMANS. SARAH O. JEWETT.
   "   "   " *PERSIA. S. G. W. BENJAMIN.
   "   "   " *SPAIN. Rev. E. E. and SUSAN HALE.
   "   "   " *GERMANY. S. BARING-GOULD.
   "   "   " THE ITALIAN REPUBLICS.
   "   "   " HOLLAND. Prof. C. E. THOROLD ROGERS.
   "   "   " *NORWAY. HJALMAR H. BOYESEN.
   "   "   " *THE MOORS IN SPAIN. STANLEY LANE-POOLE.
   "   "   " *HUNGARY. Prof. A. VÁMBÉRY.
   "   "   " THE ITALIAN KINGDOM. W. L. ALDEN.
   "   "   " EARLY FRANCE. Prof. GUSTAVE MASSON.
   "   "   " ALEXANDER'S EMPIRE. Prof. J. P. MAHAFFY.
   "   "   " THE HANSE TOWNS. HELEN ZIMMERN.
   "   "   " ASSYRIA. Z. RAGOZIN.
   "   "   " *THE SARACENS. ARTHUR GILMAN.
   "   "   " TURKEY. STANLEY LANE-POOLE.
   "   "   " PORTUGAL. H. MORSE STEPHENS.
   "   "   " MEXICO. SUSAN HALE.
   "   "   " IRELAND. Hon. EMILY LAWLESS.
   "   "   " PHŒNICIA.
   "   "   " SWITZERLAND.
   "   "   " RUSSIA.
   "   "   " WALES.
   "   "   " SCOTLAND.

* (The volumes starred are now ready, January, 1887.)

G. P. PUTNAM'S SONS

NEW YORK   LONDON
27 and 29 WEST TWENTY-THIRD STREET   27 KING WILLIAM STREET, STRAND